EMPIRE OF LIGHT

1 INT. EMPIRE CINEMA. DAY. 1

The old Empire Cinema, on the south coast of England.

It is eight o'clock in the morning on Christmas Eve, 1980. The building is empty.

A dusty morning light falls on the faded magnificence of the old Art Deco cinema. Worn plush carpets, sun-bleached curtains, red velvet ropes, gilt.

We see:

- A wide corridor disappearing into darkness. At the end of the corridor, a sign reads SCREEN ONE.

- The concessions stand - a hexagonal construction of wood, glass and chrome, sitting in the centre of the lobby.

- Grand twin staircases leading up to other levels. Ropes are hung across both staircases. Signs read 'No Entrance'.

- The Manager's office. A cold cup of tea sits on a desk.

- A small chrome box office. Light streaks in through the blinds that cover the windows. On the small counter - Christmas decorations adorn an old brass ticket machine.

- A wide expanse of glass doors. Outside the doors, snow slowly falls on the promenade and seafront.

A SILHOUETTE appears at the doors.

The silhouette is a woman. HILARY - White, mid-40s - dressed in an overcoat and gloves.

The jangling of keys as she unlocks one of the doors.

She kicks the snow off her boots, reaches over to the light switch, and the overhead lights flicker on.

2 INT. EMPIRE CINEMA. LOBBY. DAY. 2

Hilary moves across the lobby. She switches on the large Art Deco bronze chandelier that hangs above the twin staircases.

We can now see more of the faded murals and original bronzed Art Deco fantasia figures that adorn the walls.

A detail reads "*Find where light in darkness lies*".

3 INT. EMPIRE CINEMA. LOBBY. DAY. 3

She moves behind the concessions stand. Turns on the counter lights. Inside the lit glass case - Licorice Allsorts, Revels, Chewits, Flying Saucers. Packs of Silk Cut and John Player cigarettes.

She turns on the lights of a small tinsel Christmas tree.

The popcorn machine hums into life.

4 INT. EMPIRE. SCREEN 1. DAY. 4

The lights come on in sequence in the main cinema.

First, red lights mark out the aisles and stairs, then yellow and amber downlights rake the walls.

We can now see the threadbare Art Deco padded walls, the peeling paint and the faded gold of the auditorium, with its coffered ceiling and ionic columns.

In wide shot we see Hilary crossing the large auditorium. The vast empty white expanse of the sixty foot cinema screen waits behind faded velvet curtains.

5 INT. MANAGER'S OFFICE. DAY. 5

The empty Manager's Office. Hilary enters.

She tidies a cold cup of tea from the desk. Empties an ashtray. Switches on the desk lamp.

From a low drawer she pulls out a pair of men's suede slippers. Places them carefully next to the chair. Turns on the electric three bar heater.

6 INT. LOCKER ROOM. DAY. 6

A bucket in the corner catches the drips from an overhead leak.

You can still see Hilary's breath as she changes into her uniform. Purple skirt, blue blouse, purple waistcoat.

Her locker is open behind her.

Close on her name badge as she puts on her waistcoat.

Hilary Small - Duty Manager.

6A EXT. EMPIRE CINEMA - SEAFRONT. MORNING. 6A

The snow slowly floats down in front of the entrance to the building.

The lights of the large neon sign flicker on.

THE EMPIRE

And below it:

SCREEN 1 - BLUES BROTHERS SCREEN 2 - ALL THAT JAZZ

7 EXT. EMPIRE CINEMA. DAY. 7

The snowy sea front is reflected in the window of the cinema.

Hilary steps into the reflection, and we see her face clearly for the first time.

The snow falls. Solitary people walk along the front.

She looks out to sea.

Music ends.

8 INT. EMPIRE LOBBY. DAY. 8

It is a couple of hours later. The snow has stopped.

Hilary is at the concessions stand, serving a couple of teens with their arms around each other.

Hilary watches while they chat noisily. Her appearance is muted. Her manner is quiet and reserved.

TEEN GIRL (BRANDY)
...so I said 'no, piss off, you can't come, not if you're going to get off with Julie Atkins' brother again'. Silly cow.

TEEN BOY (RYAN)
Stupid cow.

BRANDY
She's such a cow.

She turns to Hilary.

BRANDY (CONT'D)
Two popcorns, please.

(CONTINUED)

8 CONTINUED: 8

HILARY
Of course. Anything else?

BRANDY
Packet of Opal Fruits.

RYAN
And a Rubber Johnny.

The girl cracks up.

Hilary flushes. She turns and busies herself with the familiar task of filling two small buckets from the popcorn machine.

She steals a glance at the couple as they kiss. Their tongues touch.

As Hilary reaches under the counter for the sweets, the sound of a man's laughter nearby. It comes from the closed door to the back office.

She looks up and sees the figure of a man through the internal window, partially obscured by slatted blinds.

Hilary turns and finishes serving the teens, and they move off.

Now we see the meagre staff, all wearing the purple uniforms. JANINE (a weekend goth in her early 20s), and TREVOR (mid 20s, skinny, shy) tear the tickets.

Elsewhere are FRANKIE (awkward, bum-fluff moustache, sweatbands) and BRIAN (spotty, small tattoo), and FINN (a chubby, long-haired rocker) all in their late teens/early 20s, and finally NEIL (bright, tall, bespectacled, mid-30s) who is manning the box office.

As Hilary wipes down the surfaces, the closed door opens, and the Manager, Mr ELLIS, steps out of the back office. He is a handsome man in his early 60s. He carries a cup of coffee.

Hilary stiffens imperceptibly as he approaches.

Ellis walks right by her without speaking.

Her eyes flick down as he passes. He wears the suede slippers.

9 INT. EMPIRE CINEMA LOBBY. DAY. 9

Afternoon now.

9 CONTINUED: 9

Hilary is standing on the landing outside Screen 1, staring off into space.

Behind her, we hear the distant sounds of a movie.

10 INT. EMPIRE CINEMA LOBBY/ENTRANCE. NIGHT. 10

Hilary is ushering out the last customers of the day. She holds the door open for them as they leave.

HILARY
Thank you... Thank you for coming...Merry Christmas...Thank you...

She closes the door behind them. Locks it.

11 INT. EMPIRE SCREEN ONE. NIGHT. 11

The hum of the velvet curtain as it closes on the big screen.

Hilary is at the back of the auditorium with her flashlight. Neil and Janine are busy tidying up litter down at the front.

They are doing the final clean up of the night.

NEIL
...and I'm not talking about a new pair of trousers. An old pair, just lying there.

JANINE
I used to do that. When my mum wouldn't let me wear my mini-skirt out of the house. Just got changed in the back row.

NEIL
Also, used nappy. Popcorn bucket with vomit inside.

JANINE
Urgh.

NEIL
A whole cooked chicken in a Safeway bag.

He calls up to Hilary at the back.

11 CONTINUED: 11

NEIL (CONT'D)
How about you, Hils? What's the worst thing you've found? Anything interesting?

HILARY
Dead body. Couple of years ago. Had a heart attack during *Smokey and the Bandit*. Took three people to move him.

JANINE
Bloody hell.

Janine and Neil look at each other, slightly horrified.

NEIL
Well, that's killed the mood.

They all laugh.

12 INT. EMPIRE. NIGHT. 12

From inside the darkened lobby, we see Hilary locking the front doors.

13 EXT. SEA FRONT. NIGHT. 13

Hilary walks along the front, the cinema behind her.

14 EXT. SEA FRONT. NIGHT. 14

We are following Hilary as she continues her journey.

Christmas lights strung between the lamp posts outline the arc of the bay in the snow.

A few Christmas revellers pass her by.

15 EXT. SEA FRONT. NIGHT. 15

Hilary crosses in front of the old Lido. The neon sign throws her shadow across the empty street.

16 EXT. QUIET SEA FRONT. NIGHT. 16

Further down the sea front now, things are quieter.

(CONTINUED)

16 CONTINUED: 16

We see Hilary's tiny figure. She is walking towards a terrace of dilapidated Georgian houses that stand looking out to sea.

17 EXT. HILARY'S APARTMENT BUILDING. NIGHT. 17

Hilary approaches the large double doors of the terrace. Above the doors it reads *Paragon Apartments*. She enters.

A light comes on in a first floor window.

In the distance, we can hear revellers.

18 INT. BEDROOM. DAY. 18

A TeasMaid gurgles next to the bed.

A pile of books sits on the bedside table.

Morning light streaks through the cracks in the curtains.

A pair of stockinged feet poke out from under the bedclothes.

An alarm goes off.

Hilary stirs.

19 INT. BATHROOM. DAY. 19

Hilary finishes brushing her teeth.

She opens the bathroom cabinet. Inside are a variety of prescription medications. She opens a bottle, shakes out two pills, places them by the sink.

She stares briefly at the pills sitting there.

She swallows them.

20 INT. KITCHEN. DAY. 20

A pre-packaged turkey breast. Some frozen peas.

Hilary prepares Christmas lunch. The radio in the background plays the Christmas Eucharist on Radio 4.

21 INT. LIVING ROOM. DAY. 21

A single Christmas cracker waits by Hilary's plate.

21 CONTINUED: 21

Cut wide to reveal Hilary's living room. The wallpaper is peeling a little, but the room is homely. Pictures, lamps, organised clutter. Bookshelves overflowing with books. Other piles of books sit on the floor.

Hilary eats Christmas lunch alone.

22 INT. LIVING ROOM. DAY. 22

Late in the day now. Hilary is sitting on the floor in front of her gas fire. She is reading a Christmas card. Smiles. She opens the attached present.

Soap. She smells it, likes it.

23 INT. BATHROOM. NIGHT. 23

Hilary lies in the bath. She soaps herself. A couple of candles provide the mood.

She slides down under the water, submerging herself fully. Gradually, her face goes under the water too.

We hold on her face.

24 INT. DOCTOR'S OFFICE. DAY. 24

It is a few days later.

Hilary sits facing DR LAIRD (60s, lean, no nonsense). Her handbag is on her lap. She has put on some lipstick.

The Doctor studies the file on the desk in front of him. The sound of seagulls outside the window.

LAIRD
Headaches? Nausea?

HILARY
No.

LAIRD
Sleeping alright?

HILARY
Yes.

LAIRD
Good.
(he looks up)
Shall we weigh you?

25 INT. DOCTOR'S OFFICE. DAY. 25

Hilary stands, shoes off, on the scales. Dr Laird peers over his glasses, writes in his notes.

LAIRD
Mmm. Not ideal. Four pounds heavier.

Hilary steps off the scales and begins to put her shoes back on.

LAIRD (CONT'D)
How do you feel? Generally?

HILARY
Fine.

LAIRD
Do you feel better since leaving St. Jude's?

HILARY
Yes.

LAIRD
Any big mood swings?

HILARY
No, not really.

LAIRD
Good. Stable. That's good.

A pause as the doctor writes a prescription.

HILARY
I do feel a bit...

She can't find the word. Dr Laird looks over his spectacles.

LAIRD
...Mmm?

HILARY
Numb. I suppose.

A beat.

LAIRD
Well, I'm sure that'll wear off as soon as you get used to the Lithium, it's marvellous stuff.

(CONTINUED)

25 CONTINUED: 25

Hilary nods. A little reassured.

Laird walks over to her and hands her the prescription.

LAIRD (CONT'D)
And you do have people you can talk to, I assume? Family, friends?

HILARY
Oh, yes.

26 INT. DANCE HALL. DAY. 26

A ballroom dancing class. Couples are paired up and already dancing.

Hilary is looking around, hopefully. An INSTRUCTOR approaches.

INSTRUCTOR
Hilary, do you have a partner?

HILARY
Yes, I... No, I don't think so.

INSTRUCTOR
Excellent - this is Bill. Bill, this is Hilary.

Hilary shakes BILL'S hand. He is in his early 80's.

BILL
How do you do.

HILARY
Lovely to meet you. Apologies in advance.

27 INT. DANCE HALL. DAY. 27

An array of old and late middle aged folks dance a foxtrot.

Hilary and Bill are amongst them.

She is struggling, but determined.

28 INT. EMPIRE. LOCKER ROOM. DAY. 28

The locker room used to be a large dressing room. Old mirrors, make-up tables, remnants of clothes hooks. Naked bulbs and chipped plaster. Lockers dotted around.

28 CONTINUED: 28

Hilary, Janine, Neil, Brian, Frankie, all laughing over lunch - sandwiches, crisps, cans of Tizer. Hilary eats a salad from a Tupperware container.

Neil has Janine's Walkman over his ears, and shouts accordingly.

NEIL
I mean, it's so depressing! He's just droning *on and on*! Wake me up when it's over!

JANINE
Piss off!

He does a passable impersonation of Joy Division's Ian Curtis, while pretending to sleepwalk.

NEIL
"Loooove...loooove will tear us apart...agaaaain"

Janine tries to grab the Walkman off him.

JANINE
(overlapping)
Don't! You're fucking... You're going to *break* it!

She finally gets it off him.

JANINE (CONT'D)
You're a tosser.

NEIL
Oooh, it's so lovely when it *stops.*

Neil laughs. Hilary is laughing despite herself.

JANINE
Yeah, whatever.

NEIL
Come back Supertramp, all is forgiven! (singing in falsetto) *"When I was young, it seemed that life was so wonderful, a miracle..."*

More laughter. A voice from the doorway:

ELLIS (O.C)
What on earth is going on in here?

(CONTINUED)

28 CONTINUED: 28

Hilary stops laughing.

NEIL
Oh sorry, Mr Ellis, Janine was playing us something on her Walkman.

ELLIS
Yes, well you can all calm down. Janine, since you're at a loose end, can you come and do tickets please? Trevor hasn't turned up again, so we're short.

JANINE
But it's my lunch break.

ELLIS
Doesn't look like you were eating much lunch.

JANINE
Well, I haven't had the chance yet.

ELLIS
My heart bleeds. Outside.

Janine huffs, but gathers up her stuff and leaves. Neil and Brian follow her. Hilary is left sitting alone at the table.

ELLIS (CONT'D)
Hilary - perhaps you and I could discuss the whole Trevor situation in my office? Ten minutes.

HILARY
Yes, of course.

He leaves.

29 INT. MANAGER'S OFFICE. DAY. 29

Hilary is wanking Mr Ellis off.

He stands awkwardly, leaning over his desk, his trousers half down. She stands behind him.

Ellis is building to a climax.

ELLIS
Suck me off.

(CONTINUED)

29 CONTINUED: 29

HILARY
No.

ELLIS
Please. Suck me.

HILARY
No. Let's keep... Like this.
Just... Like this...

Ellis's knees buckle as he comes.

They both stand breathless.

30 EXT. MANAGER'S OFFICE. DAY. 30

From outside the office, the sound of the key turning slowly in the lock.

Hilary exits, reflexively smoothing her hair.

Behind her, through the crack in the door, we see Ellis sitting at his desk, pretending to read some papers.

31 INT. CINEMA BATHROOM. DAY. 31

Hilary is washing her hands.

She stops and looks at herself in the mirror.

32 OMITTED 32

33 INT. RESTAURANT. NIGHT. 33

Hilary sits alone, with her back to the window, in a small Italian restaurant.

She finishes downing a glass of red wine. Pours herself another. Picks up her book - Iris Murdoch's *The Sea, The Sea*.

As she does this, through the window we see a couple approach the restaurant.

As they get closer, we can see that it is Mr Ellis. With him is a rather glamorous, well-dressed blonde in her mid-50s. BRENDA, his wife.

They walk up to the window and study the menu. Hilary still doesn't see them. They enter.

(CONTINUED)

33 CONTINUED: 33

Hilary looks up and spots them. She shrinks back into her chair.

The couple take their seats at a table. Brenda sits with her back to Hilary.

As Ellis sits down, he sees Hilary. He doesn't cover his shock very well. A WAITER approaches Hilary.

WAITER
May I take your order, Madam?

Hilary tries to re-focus, panicking.

HILARY
Oh, I'm not really sure. You know, I'm not... I've suddenly realised, I'm late for an appointment. I'm terribly sorry.

She puts some money down, gathers up her things, and walks out, straight past Ellis's table. Close enough to touch.

Mr Ellis doesn't look up from his menu.

34 INT. HILARY'S BEDROOM. NIGHT. 34

We are close on Hilary as she lies awake.

Her eyes flick across the ceiling as her thoughts race.

A distant dog barks.

35 EXT. SEA FRONT. DAY. 35

It is a misty morning.

Hilary walks to work, the Paragon Apartments behind her, the steel-grey sea beyond.

36 EXT. SEA FRONT. DAY. 36

Hilary approaches the cinema along the seafront. She looks up at it.

It looms up ahead of her, ominous.

37 INT. LOCKER ROOM. DAY. 37

Hilary approaches her locker. She stops, looks down.

(CONTINUED)

37 CONTINUED: 37

A brown paper bag sits by the locker.

She reaches into the bag, pulls out a box of Milk Tray chocolates.

A small note is sellotaped on top of the box. She reads:

'With deep affection. X'

She looks at the box. Angry.

38 INT. LOBBY. DAY. 38

Janine, Neil, along with Frankie and Brian and a new face, NORMAN, the projectionist (small, with dark piercing eyes, wearing jacket and tie), are all standing around the concessions stand.

Hilary remains behind the counter.

Mr Ellis is addressing them all. Next to him stands STEPHEN, a young Black man, dressed in a new purple uniform. He is about 20 - tall and slender, and unselfconsciously handsome.

Hilary watches him.

ELLIS
...so Stephen here will be replacing Trevor, who was never here anyway, so he's already off to a flying start.
(laughs at his own joke)
Anyway... this is Neil, who does Box Office mostly.

NEIL
Nice to meet you.

STEPHEN
Hiya.

ELLIS
Norman, our projectionist.

STEPHEN
Alright?

NORMAN
Hello.

(CONTINUED)

38 CONTINUED: 38

ELLIS
Janine, who'll be collecting tickets with you. Watch out for her strange musical tastes.

STEPHEN
Can't be worse than mine.

Janine laughs. She is obviously already taken with Stephen.

JANINE
Hi.

Ellis gestures down the line.

ELLIS
Frankie, Brian, and Finn with the...hair.

FRANKIE/BRIAN/FINN
Hullo/Alright/Hello.

ELLIS
And our esteemed Duty Manager Hilary, who also does sweets and snacks.

Hilary struggles to meet his eye.

HILARY
Hello.

STEPHEN
Hello.

ELLIS
So, I'll leave you all to get better acquainted. And Hilary will show you the ropes.

39 INT. CONCESSIONS STAND. DAY. 39

Close on the sweets booth at the concessions stand. A yellow box of Fruit Gums.

Hilary's hand opens the hatch, reaches in, lifts it up.

HILARY
...try and take the box at the front, otherwise it never gets sold, and then it gets dusty.

39 CONTINUED: 39

STEPHEN
Okay.
(looking back at the popcorn machine)
That smell must make you hungry. Are you never tempted to sneak a handful?

HILARY
(curtly)
No.

STEPHEN
I didn't mean steal it, I just meant-

HILARY
(interrupting)
Try and keep a tab of the number of items you sell, then replace them at the end of your shift.

She walks away.

40 INT. SCREEN ONE. DAY. 40

Hilary walks Stephen into the auditorium.

HILARY
You'll have to do final clean up if you're on late shift. Make sure you check for sleepers.

STEPHEN
Ha! Really?

HILARY
Course. We had one chap used to bring in an air mattress.

Stephen laughs. Hilary walks on.

41 INT. CINEMA CORRIDOR. DAY. 41

Hilary walks Stephen back out of Screen 1. She indicates a small single door. Stephen looks at it as they pass.

HILARY.
Projection booth. Don't go in. Norman is very particular.

She pushes through the double doors.

41A INT. CINEMA LOBBY/LANDING. DAY. 41A

Hilary comes out of the doors and starts to head down the stairs.

HILARY
You stand at the bottom of these stairs. Make sure you keep the ticket stubs, and then bring them back to me, so I can check them against admissions.

STEPHEN
Ok. When do we, you know... open up?

Hilary stops, checks her watch.

HILARY
Twenty minutes.

STEPHEN
What's up here?

He is standing by the upper staircase, with its 'No Entry' sign.

HILARY
Public aren't allowed.

STEPHEN
Can I have a look?

Hilary looks doubtful.

STEPHEN (CONT'D)
Go on. Please?

Hilary looks up to the top of the stairs.

42 OMITTED 42

43 INT. ABANDONED LOBBY/CORRIDOR. DAY. 43

A long, wide, empty corridor. The sound of keys in a lock.

At the far end of the corridor a door swings open, and Hilary and Stephen step out into...

Another lobby entirely.

(CONTINUED)

43 CONTINUED: 43

Dusty light illuminates the long since abandoned wing of the cinema.

STEPHEN
(quietly)
Oh my God. It's a whole other cinema.

HILARY
Used to be four screens.

Stephen looks around open-mouthed. They walk in silence through the old lobby.

Old posters lean against the wall. A huge old sign reads "WINES, SPIRITS AND BEERS". Dust covers everything.

43A INT. ABANDONED LOBBY/CONCESSIONS STAND. DAY. 43A

They pass an abandoned concessions stand. Smaller than the main one, but the same design.

They approach a darkened doorway.

44 INT. ABANDONED CORRIDOR. DAY. 44

Hilary has her flashlight on as they walk along a dark corridor.

They arrive at a set of double doors.

HILARY
Best for last.

And she pushes open the doors.

45 INT. ABANDONED BALLROOM. DAY. 45

The noise of the doors disturbs some pigeons, who flutter up to the roof.

It is an old ballroom.

The huge room is dominated by a large, cracked dancefloor, on which lies an ancient baby grand piano. Old booths, each with their own table and lamp, line the walls.

At the far end of the room a bar stretches the length of one wall. Above the bar, a large faded mural of a sea serpent.

(CONTINUED)

45 CONTINUED: 45

Floor to ceiling windows surround the space on three sides. Through them is an amazing view of the sea, the beach and the front.

Morning light streaks through the windows. The light catches the old velvet seats, covered in bird lime, and the dust motes swirling upwards in the air.

The beauty of the place takes Stephen's breath away.

STEPHEN
Wow. What a place.

HILARY
I know. It really was beautiful.

STEPHEN
It still is.

Hilary is struck by this. She watches Stephen as he gazes around, seeing it through his eyes.

They stand there for a moment, looking at the faded grandeur of it all.

STEPHEN (CONT'D)
Another world.

Something catches Stephen's eye.

STEPHEN (CONT'D)
Oh, look at this little fellow.

There is a sick or wounded pigeon nestling in an alcove. It makes small coo-ing noises. He reaches up.

Close: As Stephen stretches upwards, his shirt comes untucked, and Hilary can see his taut stomach above the line of his trousers.

STEPHEN (CONT'D)
I think he's broken his wing.

Hilary watches Stephen gently cradle the bird.

Suddenly, the bird flaps wildly. Hilary flinches.

STEPHEN (CONT'D)
(to the bird)
It's alright... it's alright...
sshhh.
(to Hilary)
He needs a bit of help.

46 INT. ABANDONED DINING ROOM. DAY. 46

A small private dining room, just off the ballroom. Boxes of old programmes. Film canisters sit on a workbench. Upturned chairs and stools.

The pigeon sits on a pile of boxes. A first aid box is open to one side, and Stephen is finishing tying a makeshift bandage onto its wing.

It scratches at the bandage with one of its claws, flapping with its other wing. Hilary is a little freaked out.

HILARY
Oh, he doesn't like it, he's trying to pull it off!

STEPHEN
It's ok, he's fine.

The pigeon settles. Stephen holds him out to Hilary.

STEPHEN (CONT'D)
Here. Hold him.

HILARY
Oh, no. No, I don't like birds. No.

STEPHEN
Come on. Look... like this.

Hilary hesitantly allows Stephen to take her hands, and gently put them on the bird. Before she knows it, she is softly holding him.

STEPHEN (CONT'D)
There you go! He loves it... He prefers you.

Hilary is stupidly pleased. She holds him carefully.

STEPHEN (CONT'D)
Now...

Stephen reaches down, takes off his shoe and his sock.

HILARY
What you doing?

He cuts a couple of holes in the sock with the scissors, ties a knot in the other end, and slips it over the pigeon's head.

STEPHEN
Special trick.

(CONTINUED)

46 CONTINUED: 46

The pigeon's head pops out of one hole, and its two feet stick out of the holes at the other end. The effect is cute and comical.

STEPHEN (CONT'D)
You can put him down now.

Hilary lets the bird stand on the boxes. The bird hops around.

Stephen watches Hilary laugh. Her face lit up.

HILARY
What happens when he needs the loo?

They both laugh.

47 INT. SUPERMARKET. DAY. 47

Hilary is moving down a supermarket aisle.

Her trolley has a few things in it. She stops. Reaches up. Takes a bottle of Babycham from the shelf. Studies the price. Puts it in her trolley.

48 INT. LOCKER ROOM. DAY. 48

The bottle of Babycham stands on the table in the middle of the room. A Tupperware box of yellow cupcakes sits next to it.

Hilary sits at the table with a cup of tea - money box and piles of ticket stubs in front of her - writing the ticket sales onto a xeroxed sheet. She has put on some lipstick.

Norman sits doing the crossword in the corner.

NORMAN
Nine across, five letters: 'A word that starts a Waste Land'?

A beat.

HILARY
April.

NORMAN
(to himself)
Ha.

Norman fills in the answer. Neil enters.

48 CONTINUED: 48

NEIL
Morning Hils.

HILARY
Morning.

NEIL
Have you got your glad rags for tonight?

HILARY
Yes. And I brought those in for later.

She indicates the bottle and the cupcakes.

NEIL
Ooh, I say!

Janine and Stephen come into the room, mid-conversation. Frankie and Brian follow.

JANINE
...so, we could go down Misty's off Tivoli Road, if we can get in. Or that club Hades at the Lido has got a good DJ.

STEPHEN
Yeah, maybe, yeah.

Stephen hangs his black suit on a hook, and puts his shoes and his pork pie hat into his locker.

Much of this dialogue overlaps. Frankie and Brian are also chatting in the background.

Hilary continues with her task. She doesn't necessarily watch the others, but she is very aware of them, especially Stephen.

NEIL
What's all that?

STEPHEN
(holding up his hat and suit)
It's my stingy brim. And my three button Tonic. For tonight.

NEIL
Didn't have you down as a Rude Boy!

48 CONTINUED: 48

NORMAN
(to Stephen)
What you going on about?

STEPHEN
Two-Tone.

NORMAN
Who-tone?

STEPHEN
You know, *Two-Tone*! The Specials, The Selecter, The Beat.

NORMAN
I don't understand a single thing you're saying to me.

Stephen laughs.

JANINE
It's a bit like reggae, but dance music. Fast reggae.

NEIL
(trying on Stephen's hat in the mirror)
Always fancied one of these.

STEPHEN
Yeah, you've got the reggae ska side, and then you've got the punk side. Black and White together. It's a melting pot.

JANINE
(starts singing The Specials)
'You done too much, much too young'

Stephen joins in, serenading Norman.

JANINE/STEPHEN
'You're married with a kid when you could be having fun with meee...!'

NORMAN
God help us.

STEPHEN
What about you Hilary? Going to come dancing with us?

(CONTINUED)

48 CONTINUED: 48

HILARY
Oh, I'm not sure about that. Not my thing, really.

NORMAN
Discotheques. What a bloody nightmare.

Stephen has moved near to Hilary to put on his waistcoat. Hilary is very aware of his presence.

STEPHEN
So what you going to do?

Hilary looks up.

HILARY
Thought I might go up onto the roof to watch the fireworks.

STEPHEN
Nice.

NORMAN
(to Stephen)
Where's all *your* mates, anyway?

STEPHEN
Buggered off to college.

JANINE
(re: college)
That's where I'm going.

NORMAN
Good luck with that.

Stephen has finished doing up his waistcoat.

STEPHEN
Off we go, then. Another day, another four pounds fifty!

Stephen heads out the door. Janine stares after him.

JANINE
(to Neil)
Oh my God. He is *such* a *much* of a *hunk*.

Neil laughs as Janine follows Stephen out of the door.

(CONTINUED)

48 CONTINUED: 48

NEIL
(re: Janine and Stephen)
Now *that...* is on the cards.

Hilary forces a smile.

HILARY
Mmm.

Neil leaves.

49 INT. LADIES TOILET. EMPIRE. DAY. 49

Hilary comes in through the door. Goes to the mirror. Looks at herself. She is flushed. She wipes her lipstick off.

HILARY
(to herself)
Embarrassing.

50 INT. LOBBY. CONCESSIONS STAND. DAY. 50

The popcorn machine is making a small avalanche of popcorn. Hilary fills a bucket, hands it to a CUSTOMER. She hears a giggling across the lobby. She looks up.

Janine and Stephen are taking tickets, laughing at some private joke.

Hilary watches them.

An OLD MAN (MR PODD) presents his ticket to Stephen. Stephen tears it. Then, as Mr Podd climbs the stairs to Screen 1, Stephen does a little impersonation of his shuffling, hunchbacked walk. Janine stifles hysterics.

Hilary continues to watch, unamused.

51 INT. LOBBY. UNDER STAIRS. NIGHT. 51

It's later. Hilary is at the cupboard under the stairs, tidying away the velvet rope and brass stanchions.

Stephen puts his head around the door.

STEPHEN
That's the eight o'clock up and running.

Hilary ignores him.

(CONTINUED)

STEPHEN (CONT'D)
So what time you clocking off?

HILARY
Where are the ticket stubs?

STEPHEN
I gave them to Janine.

HILARY
(looking around)
And where is Janine?

STEPHEN
Shit. I think she went early.

A beat. Hilary stares at him.

HILARY
You had *one* thing I asked you to do. *One thing*.

STEPHEN
Yeah, I know, but I thought that I could-

HILARY
(suddenly raising her voice)
It's just not acceptable!

A beat of shock.

STEPHEN
Alright, it's... there's no need to shout.

HILARY
It's completely unprofessional... and, and impersonating the customers, laughing behind their backs!
(really shouting now)
People come here for a nice time, not to be laughed at!

A beat while Stephen takes this in.

STEPHEN
Yeah, you're right. I'm sorry.

HILARY
(calmer now)
Good. Just...

51 CONTINUED: 51

A pause.

HILARY (CONT'D)
Don't laugh at people.

She walks off.

52 EXT/INT. EMPIRE BOX OFFICE. NIGHT. 52

It is night. The lights of the Empire sign glow, and various New Year's Eve revellers sing their way along the seafront.

We can see Hilary, who is inside the box office, which is at the front of the building and faces directly out onto the street. She stares out at the sea front, distracted.

Nearby, Neil is finishing changing the small sign on the back of the box office wall that announces the day's movie times ('Dolly Parton in NINE TO FIVE - showings at 12.30pm, 3.30pm, 6pm, 9pm') and changing the letters, so they read:

'WELCOME 1981! - HAPPY NEW YEAR TO ALL OUR LOYAL CUSTOMERS!'

Mr Ellis pokes his head around the door.

ELLIS
Hilary. When you're done later, why don't you pop into the office for a quick drink?

HILARY
Oh, I don't know...

ELLIS
Come on, just for a minute. Toast the New Year.

HILARY
Alright. That would be nice.

Ellis leaves. A beat. Neil looks at her, she avoids his gaze.

NEIL
No invite for *me*, I see.

Hilary flushes, and ignores him.

53 INT. MANAGER'S OFFICE. NIGHT. 53

The lights are off in the office. We can see a streetlit alleyway through the window.

(CONTINUED)

53 CONTINUED: 53

Ellis and Hilary are kissing in the semi-darkness. In the background we can hear the bass thump of the movie soundtrack playing through the wall.

Ellis begins to lift Hilary's skirt. She pushes it back down.

They speak in whispers.

HILARY
I can't. This is all wrong.

They struggle a bit more. Ellis puts his hand between her legs.

HILARY (CONT'D)
Stop it!

She pushes Ellis away, pulls her skirt down. Ellis stands there, a little breathless.

ELLIS
Why? Who is this hurting?

HILARY
Well, your wife, for one.

ELLIS
She has no idea.

HILARY
That doesn't mean it's-

ELLIS
(interrupting)
Look. Brenda doesn't know me anymore. We've been sleeping in different rooms since last summer. She won't even make me a cup of tea.
(he approaches her, begins kissing her neck)
And you are just the most... wonderful person (kiss) so helpful ...(kiss) I feel such tenderness towards you...(kiss)

He pulls her in to an embrace. Hilary is reluctantly allowing herself to be taken over by it.

ELLIS (CONT'D)
...and your arse feels so good in my hands.

53 CONTINUED: 53

Ellis starts to lift her skirt, and push her back onto the desk.

She resigns herself to it.

54 INT. MANAGER'S OFFICE. LATER. 54

Close on two large tumblers of whisky being poured.

Ellis lifts them both, hands one to Hilary. Hilary is still flushed. Ellis is smoking a slim Panatella. The lights are now on.

ELLIS
Well... here's to 1981.

They clink glasses. Hilary takes a steadying gulp.

ELLIS (CONT'D)
Lovely stuff that. Glenfiddich.

HILARY
Mmm.

She takes another gulp. Ellis puts his stockinged feet up on the coffee table.

ELLIS
Any new year's resolutions?

She looks at him for a beat. She wants to say: 'To end this affair'.

HILARY
No, not really. Eat a bit better, maybe. Also I thought I might-

ELLIS
(interrupting)
I'd like to expand this place a little. Get it on the map.
(he takes a sip)
Can I let you in on a secret? You musn't tell anyone.

HILARY
What?

ELLIS
It looks like we might get a big South Coast premiere. The Mayor, Councillors, South Coast Herald, the lot.

(CONTINUED)

54 CONTINUED: 54

HILARY
Gosh that's... that would be wonderful.

ELLIS
I know. *Chariots Of Fire*. That's the film. It was between us and the Odeon, but they didn't want a circuit cinema, and it looks like we've got the nod. So we'll have to spruce the place up a bit.

He looks at her.

ELLIS (CONT'D)
Could be the beginning of an exciting new chapter.

He lets this hang a moment.

Hilary downs the rest of her whisky.

55 INT. EMPIRE LOBBY. NIGHT. 55

Hilary is alone in the empty lobby. She is turning off the various lights in the concessions stand. You can sense from her movements that she is now slightly drunk.

She goes behind the concessions stand, looks down.

HILARY
Oh, no.

On the carpet at her feet is a dropped ice cream cone, melted.

She stares at it. Then suddenly, a loud knock on the front window. Hilary jumps out of her skin.

HILARY (CONT'D)
Jesus!

Another knock.

HILARY (CONT'D)
(calling)
Hello?

STEPHEN (O.S.)
It's me. Stephen.

She goes over, turns on the exterior overhead lights. We now can see Stephen dressed in his suit and hat.

(CONTINUED)

55 CONTINUED: 55

STEPHEN (CONT'D)
Hiya.

HILARY
I'm just locking up.

She opens the door.

STEPHEN
I wanted to apologise for earlier.

HILARY
Oh, it's fine. Really. (beat) I'm sorry I shouted. Come in.

He steps into the darkness of the lobby, the door closes behind him. They are standing close to each other.

HILARY (CONT'D)
Why didn't you go with Janine?

STEPHEN
I did, for a bit. But I don't know any of her mates, and people were...y'know...staring. So.

A beat while Hilary registers this.

HILARY
How awful to feel watched.

STEPHEN
(brushing it off)
Yeah, sometimes. (beat) Anyway, I thought you might want company. Up on the roof.

Hilary's heart skips a beat.

HILARY
Oh, I'd almost forgotten.

She smiles, looks at him. She is a little drunk.

HILARY (CONT'D)
Yes, alright. Why not?

56 EXT. EMPIRE ROOFTOP. NIGHT. 56

Hilary and Stephen walk out of a small door onto the roof. The neon Empire sign lights them both.

(CONTINUED)

56 CONTINUED: 56

The rooftops and seafront stretch out before them. In the distance, the sea.

STEPHEN
What a view...

They both look out across the rooftops.

Stephen looks up to see a huge towerblock looming up in the middle distance.

STEPHEN (CONT'D)
And look at that. If I had some binoculars, I could almost see my mum.

HILARY
Is that where you live?

STEPHEN
Yeah.

A beat. He is slightly embarrassed.

STEPHEN (CONT'D)
Do you always come up here New Year's Eve?

HILARY
Last couple of years.

STEPHEN
Don't blame you.

They stand awkwardly for a moment.

She holds up the Babycham.

HILARY
Here...

She pops the cork. Pours it into two paper cups from the concession stand.

HILARY (CONT'D)
Not exactly Moët, but better than Tizer.

She hands Stephen a cup.

HILARY (CONT'D)
Sorry it's just us.

56 CONTINUED: 56

STEPHEN
No, this is nice. (beat) I'm not really a fan of New Year's Eve, anyway. Last year I puked on my new shoes.

HILARY
(laughs)
Oh no! What happened to them?

Stephen lifts his leg to show a tasseled shoe.

STEPHEN
They survived.

He holds up his paper cup.

STEPHEN (CONT'D)
Cheers.

HILARY
Cheers.

She takes a small sip of Babycham.

STEPHEN
Come on! Get it down you!

HILARY
(giggling)
I'm not sure I should. I've already had too much.

STEPHEN
Really? When?

Hilary doesn't answer.

STEPHEN (CONT'D)
Oh, come on. (American accent)'What are you, a woman or a wouse?'

HILARY
(puzzled)
What's that?

STEPHEN
Nine to Five.

Hilary doesn't understand.

STEPHEN (CONT'D)
You know, *Nine to Five*, the film we're showing.

HILARY
(understanding)
Aah...

STEPHEN
Honestly, anyone would think you worked in a bank, Hilary. Why don't you sneak in and watch?

HILARY
No, no, that's for the customers. And it gets so busy out front, always so much to do...
(she stops)
Oh God listen to me, I'm so *boring*.

They both laugh.

HILARY (CONT'D)
Honestly...

She lifts her cup, takes a longer drink. He drinks too. Down below, the clock bells start to chime across the town.

HILARY (CONT'D)
Listen.

They walk closer to the edge of the roof in order to hear the chiming of the bells. They stand listening for a beat, looking out over the sea.

HILARY (CONT'D)
(quietly)
Ring out, wild bells, to the wild sky,
The flying cloud, the frosty light:
The year is dying in the night;
Ring out, wild bells, and let him die.

A beat.

STEPHEN
That's nice.

HILARY
Tennyson.

Stephen looks at her, impressed. That was unexpected.

In the distance, the sound of the New Year countdown.

They smile and join in.

56 CONTINUED: 56

HILARY/STEPHEN
...Eight...seven...six...five...
four...three...two...one... Happy
New Year!

Suddenly, distant car horns, cheering, and above them and all around them... *fireworks*.

The fireworks explode over the rooftops and the front, reflecting in the sea. It's genuinely beautiful.

They both stand staring.

Hilary turns and takes a long look at Stephen, who is watching the lights cascade around him.

Then... she takes her life in her hands, and kisses him.

He is surprised at first, but then he reciprocates.

They break. Stare at each other for a beat. She seems as surprised as him.

HILARY
Shit.

She turns and leaves.

STEPHEN
Where you going?

Hilary keeps walking, gets to the door. Stephen calls after her.

STEPHEN (CONT'D)
It's alright!

But she's gone.

Stephen stands alone, with the fireworks still going off around him.

57 INT. DANCE HALL. DAY. 57

The dance class. It is late afternoon and the sun is low.

Through the windows, we see the dancers spinning across the floor in a collective amateur waltz. It is strangely beautiful to watch.

Through the spinning bodies, we see Hilary.

(CONTINUED)

57 CONTINUED: 57

This time she is more engaged, less self-conscious, and lost in the music. We watch her dance for a while.

58 INT. CHEMIST'S. DAY. 58

Hilary is trying out perfumes in the Chemist's shop.

She sprays her wrist and sniffs it. Likes it.

She looks up. On the pavement outside the shop she spots Stephen, presumably heading into work.

59 EXT. CHEMIST'S/STREET. DAY. 59

Hilary exits the Chemist's holding a small bag. Stephen is up ahead. She isn't quite sure how to play it, so she begins to follow him. She walks a few paces behind him, willing him to turn, to spot her.

As she follows, she begins to watch his easy walk, his shoulders, his physical beauty.

She follows him down some steps, and out onto the front.

Up ahead, Stephen is now walking under the old colonnades, set back from the seafront.

Three skinheads (COLIN, MIKEY and SEAN) sit in the shadows, smoking, holding cans of lager. A fourth skinhead (POGO) dances to his own private music, off his head on glue and marching powder.

Colin and Mikey call out to Stephen.

SKINHEAD 1 (COLIN)

Oi..!

Stephen doesn't respond. Behind him, Hilary slows.

COLIN

OI!

Still no response. They are walking towards him.

Hilary stops and watches. Colin and Mikey are now flanking Stephen. They are clearly saying things into his ear, but Hilary can't hear. The atmosphere is threatening.

Stephen keeps moving. They are beginning to push and jostle him. Sean has joined them.

59 CONTINUED: 59

COLIN (CONT'D)
Go home then, you fucking Coon!

They start making monkey noises, following him up the street.

SKINHEADS
Oo-Oo-Oo.

As they approach the end of the colonnades, one of them trips Stephen from behind. Hilary watches as he stumbles, but keeps walking.

Then two POLICEMEN appear up ahead, walking towards them down the slope.

The three skinheads spot the police and peel off.

The last one left is Colin. He says something into Stephen's ear, and walks away.

Stephen walks on.

Hilary seems paralysed. She stands and watches him go.

60 INT. LOCKER ROOM. DAY. 60

Stephen sits, subdued, now dressed in his uniform.

Hilary has also changed, and sits watching him out of the corner of her eye. Meanwhile, Norman holds forth to Neil.

NORMAN
I told management months ago, there should be a no smoking rule in *both* auditoria. Smoke compromises the viewing experience - it ruins the projected image, and it stains the screen. Simple common sense...

Hilary is still watching Stephen. He doesn't lift his gaze.

NORMAN (CONT'D)
...all I'm saying - a certain degree of specialist knowledge is essential. You need to understand basic optical and mechanical principles to be in this game. Like I told Ellis - any old numpty can sell tickets.

Ellis has walked in, all business.

60 CONTINUED: 60

NORMAN (CONT'D)
(sheepish)
Oh, hello, Mr Ellis.

ELLIS
Morning Norman, morning all.
Hilary, can you pop in for a
moment?

HILARY
No.

A beat.

ELLIS
I'm sorry?

HILARY
No, I can't. I'm running late
already. I need to open up.

ELLIS
(unamused)
Alright, suit yourself.

Stephen has looked up from across the room, surprised at Hilary's tone.

Ellis leaves. A beat.

Almost immediately, Ellis comes back in.

ELLIS (CONT'D)
I was going to ask you to stay late
tonight. Brenda and I have an
engagement, so I need to be gone by
six. *Sorry*.

He leaves again.

Stephen looks across at Hilary. Her eyes fill with tears.

61 INT. LOBBY. DAY. 61

Stephen is quietly taking the last of the customers' tickets.

He looks across at Hilary wiping down the concessions stand. He walks over to her.

STEPHEN
I think our little friend might
need a visit.

(CONTINUED)

61 CONTINUED: 61

Hilary looks at him quizzically.

STEPHEN (CONT'D)
Cheer him up.

62 INT. ABANDONED BALLROOM. DAY. 62

They walk into the Ballroom. This is clearly where the pigeon has been recuperating.

They separate and look around, searching for the pigeon in the dusk. Stephen looks over in one corner.

Hilary looks over by the bar. She looks up at the mural - the sea serpent looms over her.

Then a small coo-ing noise from behind the bar.

HILARY
Here he is.

The pigeon hops around on the floor behind the bar, still dressed in his sock.

Hilary bends down and picks him up.

HILARY (CONT'D)
Hello.

63 INT. ABANDONED DINING ROOM. DAY. 63

A few moments later. They are in the old private dining room that adjoins the ballroom, standing by an open window.

Hilary is watching as Stephen unpeels the last of the bandage from the bird's wing. She watches Stephen's face as he does this.

The bird gingerly flaps his wings. Stephen gently holds him by his legs, squinting at him.

STEPHEN
Look...at...that. Good as new.

HILARY
Amazing.

They move to the window.

STEPHEN
(to the bird)
Time to say goodbye.

(CONTINUED)

63 CONTINUED: 63

The pigeon flaps a bit...and then just takes off, flying into the evening sky.

HILARY
Bye...

They watch him go, standing next to each other at the window.

HILARY (CONT'D)
(filled with longing)
To be able to fly.

STEPHEN
(quietly)
Yeah.

They turn to face each other. Look at each other for a moment. Then they kiss. Long, and increasingly passionate.

They back up against the wall.

It all happens quickly. We see only Hilary's face as Stephen pulls down her knickers.

Hilary gasps as he enters her.

They fuck like that, against the wall.

Her hands reach up and clasp the back of his head.

64 INT. ABANDONED BALLROOM. NIGHT. 64

It is night now. Stephen and Hilary are both sitting, feet up, at an old booth.

Hilary's flashlight is on. It makes a pool of light in the centre of the huge room. Streetlights throw strange shadows on the wall.

They are mid-conversation. They both smoke.

STEPHEN
...Trinidad originally. They brought my mum over in the Sixties to train as a nurse. Apparently they needed workers. 'Help rebuild the mother country, make your fortune!'. (He laughs) She's still here, still a nurse.

HILARY
Ah, so that explains the pigeon splint...

(CONTINUED)

64 CONTINUED: 64

STEPHEN
(smiling)
You got me.

HILARY
And here was me thinking you were Jesus.

He laughs.

HILARY (CONT'D)
What about your dad?

STEPHEN
He was a bus driver. But he left years ago.

HILARY
Where to?

STEPHEN
Don't know.

HILARY
Gosh. How did you feel?

STEPHEN
(quickly)
Fine.

He looks away.

STEPHEN (CONT'D)
It's always been just me and my mum. (beat) She's the best.

HILARY
Wish I could say the same for mine.

A pause. Hilary takes a drag on her cigarette.

Stephen looks across at her.

STEPHEN
(re: the sex)
Was that... you know? (beat) Was it ok?

Hilary is quietly surprised.

HILARY
(warmly)
Yes. (beat) It was more than ok.

64 CONTINUED: 64

They look at each other. Then she suddenly remembers something.

HILARY (CONT'D)
Shit. What time is it?

65 INT. TWIN STAIRCASES. NIGHT. 65

Hilary comes rushing down the staircase into the lobby. Neil is waiting for her by the box office.

NEIL
Where have you been? Ellis left ten minutes ago, he said you were covering.

HILARY
I'm so sorry.

Hilary hurries across the lobby towards Neil.

NEIL
I've had to keep them all waiting outside! And where's Stephen?

HILARY
I don't know...
(looking around unconvincingly)
Is he not here?

She moves off to let the customers in.

Then, a voice from the stairs.

STEPHEN (O.S.)
Sorry!

Neil turns to see Stephen also coming down the top stairs. Neil turns and looks at Hilary, and back at Stephen, putting two and two together.

Stephen can't meet his gaze.

Neil turns and walks away.

66 INT. ROLLER RINK. FAIRGROUND. DAY. 66

The Roller Rink is a remnant of disco days.

Stephen, Hilary and Janine are out on the rink, sliding and skidding amateurishly.

(CONTINUED)

66 CONTINUED: 66

Janine is good at it. Hilary is better than Stephen and has some grace. But Stephen is hopeless. He attempts a spin, and falls flat on his backside. Janine and Hilary both laugh.

Around them, a few people stare.

66A EXT. FAIRGROUND. DAY. 66A *

Hilary, Stephen and Janine ride the Twister at the fairground. They are all laughing. *
*

67 EXT. CANDYFLOSS STALL. FAIRGROUND. DAY. 67

Stephen, Janine and Hilary buying candyfloss from a stall at the fairground.

While Janine is being served and paying, Hilary looks over to Stephen.

They meet each other's eye. They smile a private smile.

67A EXT. FAIRGROUND. DAY. 67A

Stephen and Hilary walk through the fairground, holding their now half-eaten candyfloss. The old roller coaster in the background.

They are mid-conversation.

HILARY
Why not?

STEPHEN
Because it's pointless. They turned me down the first time.

HILARY
To study what?

STEPHEN
Architecture.

HILARY
Oh, that would have been wonderful.

STEPHEN
(wistful)
Yeah.

HILARY
Well...you need to try again.

(CONTINUED)

67A CONTINUED: 67A

STEPHEN
(unconvinced)
Yeah, maybe.

(CONTINUED)

67A CONTINUED: 67A

HILARY
You can't just give up.

Stephen says nothing.

HILARY (CONT'D)
Stephen.

They stop. Stephen looks at her.

HILARY (CONT'D)
Don't let them tell you what you can and can't do. No one's going to *give* you the life you want. You have to go out and get it.

She looks at him intently.

HILARY (CONT'D)
You mustn't stay here.

Something in the way she says this galvanises Stephen. He looks at her, nods.

STEPHEN
Alright.

Hilary smiles.

68 INT. HILARY'S BEDROOM/BATHROOM. MORNING. 68

Next morning. Hilary opens the curtains. Light streams in.

Music is on in the background as Hilary brushes her hair. She seems light, untroubled.

We watch her move into the bathroom. She puts down the hairbrush and opens the bathroom cabinet. Takes out her medication.

She stops herself. Looks at the bottle.

She puts it back on the shelf. Unopened.

Closes the cabinet.

69 INT. LOBBY. LATE MORNING. 69

The lobby is quite busy. Stephen is standing, tearing tickets.

(CONTINUED)

69 CONTINUED: 69

MR COOPER - a regular in his sixties - approaches Stephen and hands him his ticket. He is eating some chips wrapped in newspaper and carrying a white polystyrene cup filled with milk.

STEPHEN
(tearing his ticket)
I'm sorry, Sir. You'll have to finish those out here, you can't bring them in.

COOPER
Why not?

STEPHEN
Because those are the rules.

COOPER
S'my breakfast.

STEPHEN
I know, but you've got a couple of minutes before the film starts, so...

COOPER
I'll miss the Coming Attractions.

STEPHEN
Well, it's up to you.

COOPER
Are you fucking serious?

Beat.

STEPHEN
Yes.

Cooper looks at Janine, and across to Hilary. A small queue has now formed behind Mr Cooper.

COOPER
Are you going to stand there and let me be bossed around by this...

It hangs in the air.

STEPHEN
By this what?
(beat)
By this *what*?

Mr Cooper stares at him.

(CONTINUED)

69 CONTINUED: 69

Hilary steps in.

HILARY
Alright now, Mr Cooper. You haven't got many chips left, look. You can eat a few and give the rest to me.

She holds out her hand for the chips.

HILARY (CONT'D)
I love a chip.

Mr Cooper turns to Stephen and shoves a handful of chips into his mouth. He chews them slowly, looking at Stephen. Stephen doesn't break his gaze.

Mr Cooper swallows. Hands the remains of the bag of chips to Hilary. Slowly drinks his milk. Finishes it. Hands the empty cup to Hilary.

Stephen still doesn't break eye contact.

COOPER
(to Stephen)
Happy now?

Stephen controls himself, steps aside and Mr Cooper walks in.

A beat of silence.

HILARY
I'm sorry Stephen. He's always a bit of a handful.

JANINE
He's a dickhead.

Stephen says nothing.

JANINE (CONT'D)
You ok?

Stephen stands there in silence. Then suddenly he turns and walks out.

Hilary calls out after him.

HILARY
Stephen? Stephen!

70 EXT. SEAFRONT. DAY. 70

Hilary runs up behind Stephen, putting on her coat. Her voice is raised against the wind.

HILARY
Stephen!

Stephen is walking fast along the front. His hands shake as he tries to light a cigarette. The wind from the sea is strong. She catches up with him.

HILARY (CONT'D)
There's no point in walking out.

STEPHEN
There's every point.

He strides ahead.

HILARY
He's just an angry man. He's always angry about something.

STEPHEN
Look, I know you're trying to help, Hilary, but you're just making it worse.

HILARY
(incredulous)
How am I making it worse?

STEPHEN
By pretending it isn't there.

HILARY
I really don't know what you're talking about.

Stephen stops, and turns to face her.

STEPHEN
(with intensity)
Alright, put it this way - *he's not just "angry", is he*?

Hilary stares back at him.

STEPHEN (CONT'D)
(shaking with emotion)
He should be the one to leave. Not me.

(CONTINUED)

70 CONTINUED: 70

Stephen turns and walks on.

Hilary catches him up again.

HILARY
You're absolutely right, Stephen.
I'm sorry.

Stephen nods, slowing down.

HILARY (CONT'D)
Really.

They walk a bit further.

HILARY (CONT'D)
Alright, I think this might be the moment to demonstrate one of my great talents.

Stephen looks at her.

71 EXT. TIDEPOOL BEACH. DAY. 71

A stone skims across the water.

Hilary and Stephen are standing skimming stones at a tidepool on the empty windswept beach.

HILARY
...does it happen a lot?

STEPHEN
More than it used to. Especially the last few months.

HILARY
Really? Why?

Stephen laughs, slightly incredulous.

HILARY (CONT'D)
What's funny?

STEPHEN
Well, it's everywhere, isn't it?

Hilary looks at him questioningly. She has no idea.

HILARY
Is it?

STEPHEN
Yes, it is. All that stuff in Brixton. And skinheads. And Thatcher. And those kids in New Cross.

HILARY
What was New Cross?

STEPHEN
It was in the news a couple of weeks ago. This girl's sixteenth birthday party. Someone started a fire, they reckon it was the National Front. The stairs collapsed. Sixty people trapped, children, teenagers. No one came for them, no police, nothing. (beat) They had to jump out of a second-floor window. It was so hot, people's skin was peeling back. So they jumped. Thirteen kids dead, more than fifty injured. (beat) No one came.

We see Hilary's face. She is shocked. He throws a stone.

STEPHEN (CONT'D)
It's not going away.

He throws another.

HILARY
I told you - you have to hold it sideways.

He looks at her, rolls his eyes and then skims one. It skips across the waves. A beauty.

HILARY (CONT'D)
Alright, not bad. Still some training needed. Watch this.

Hilary throws a stone. Plop. Stephen turns and smiles.

HILARY (CONT'D)
Ok I was lying, I'm shit at it.

Stephen laughs.

HILARY (CONT'D)
Kiss me.

Stephen looks around.

(CONTINUED)

71 CONTINUED: 71

HILARY (CONT'D)
Go on. No one's looking. Kiss me.

They kiss.

The gulls wheel and circle overhead.

72 OMITTED 72

73 EXT. ALLEYWAY OUTSIDE CINEMA. DAY. 73

Norman and Stephen stand waiting in the alleyway alongside the cinema. They both smoke.

A van pulls in. On the side of the van is written FTS - FILM TRANSPORT SERVICES. They open the doors, revealing several large piles of metal film canisters.

NORMAN
Lift them carefully - it's precious cargo. And only take four canisters at a time, 'cos they are not light.

Stephen leans into the van and lifts them.

74 INT. LOBBY LANDING. DAY. 74

Hilary is sitting on the landing outside Screen 1 filling in the forms for the week's new films, as Norman and Stephen climb the stairs with the film canisters.

As they walk past her, Stephen looks at her and opens his eyes wide, as if to say "this is exciting!". She smiles.

75 INT. PROJECTION BOOTH. DAY. 75

The door of the projection booth opens and they push inside.

NORMAN
You can put them down there.

Stephen lowers the canisters carefully onto the floor, as Norman busies himself making tea.

Stephen looks around. The booth is split into two rooms. The first room has a work bench along one wall, and a small sink, various utensils, mugs, a kettle etc.

(CONTINUED)

75 CONTINUED: 75

The walls and ceiling of this room are almost entirely covered with photographs cut out from magazines and newspapers. Movie stars, directors. Staring back at Stephen are Cary Grant, Hitchcock, Billy Wilder, Truffaut, Grace Kelly, Fellini, Bette Davis, Peter Sellers, Jane Fonda, Peckinpah, Jeanne Moreau, Bergman, Bob Fosse.

There is a small internal window onto a second, smaller space. In this room sit the projectors. Norman sees Stephen staring.

NORMAN (CONT'D)
You can go in if you want.

Stephen enters. In the middle of the tiny low-ceilinged room, two enormous 35mm projectors.

Pinned to the wall between the projectors, a small black and white snapshot of a little boy, about seven years old.

Stephen leans in and looks at it, but says nothing.

Norman enters behind him. He pats one of the projectors, as you would a horse.

NORMAN (CONT'D)
These are my babies. Pair of Model 18 Kalees.

STEPHEN
I had no idea they would be so big.

Norman hands him his tea.

NORMAN
Well, that's just as it should be. You don't *want* people to know. They should just see a beam of light. But back here... belts, straps, pulleys, intermittents, sprockets. It's a machine.

Stephen gets closer to it, squinting to see the workings.

76 INT. LOBBY LANDING. DAY. 76

Outside on the landing, Hilary has finished her task. She turns and looks at the closed doors. A little jealous.

77 INT. PROJECTION BOOTH. DAY. 77

Stephen is looking through an open hatch at the side of the projector. *

STEPHEN
What's this?

NORMAN
That's the carbons.

Stephen looks puzzled.

NORMAN (CONT'D)
The spark between the carbons makes the light. And nothing happens without light.

He takes out a box of rolling tobacco and some papers. *

NORMAN (CONT'D)
Ciggy?

STEPHEN
No thanks.

Norman rolls a cigarette, lights it. He opens the little *
projection window into the auditorium and blows the smoke out *
of the hatch.

Stephen is still scrutinising the projector.

STEPHEN (CONT'D)
Amazing.

NORMAN
It is amazing. Because it's just *
static frames, with darkness in *
between. But there's a little flaw *
in your optic nerve, so that if I *
run the film at 24 frames per *
second, you don't see the darkness. *

STEPHEN
Wow.

He takes a drag of his cigarette.

NORMAN
'The Phi Phenomenon'. Viewing static images rapidly in succession creates an illusion of motion.

(CONTINUED)

77 CONTINUED: 77

He turns to Stephen, who is spellbound.

NORMAN (CONT'D)
An illusion of life.

78 INT. LOBBY LANDING. DAY. 78

Hilary still waits. The door from Screen 1 opens. Stephen comes out and heads down the stairs. Hilary catches him up.

HILARY
(sotto)
What was that about?

STEPHEN
(eyes wide)
I don't know, but it was *amazing*.

79 INT. SCREEN ONE. AUDITORIUM. DAY. 79

Mr Ellis stands on stage in front of the big screen, addressing the staff. Next to him stands JIM BOOTH (sweaty, officious) from the Mayor's office. He holds a clip-board.

Stephen, Neil and Janine sit together in the auditorium, watching them. Hilary sits one row back, half watching Stephen. Norman and the rest of the staff are scattered about.

ELLIS
So on top of giving the lobby a lick of paint and all the rest, we're going to need special signage, red carpet, and crash barriers for the crowd. I think the Mayor's office will provide some security, Jim?

BOOTH
Indeed. There will be a small security detail. You can expect the Mayor of course, and his entourage, which is not insubstantial. We're waiting for confirmation, but guests look to include...
(reading from the clip-board)
Dora Bryan, Sir Laurence Olivier, Steve Ovett, Dame Flora Robson, Dusty Springfield, and possibly Paul McCartney.

(CONTINUED)

79 CONTINUED: 79

A ripple of excitement.

ELLIS
Goodness.

BOOTH
Yes, I know.
(to Ellis)
Lives in Rye.

80 EXT. EMPIRE. NIGHT. 80

It's later. Hilary, Janine, Neil and Stephen come spilling out of the cinema, chatting excitedly.

81 INT. DOCTOR'S OFFICE. DAY. 81

Hilary has just got off the scales, and is putting her shoes back on. Dr Laird is consulting his notes.

LAIRD
Two pounds down since last time.
Well done.

HILARY
Yes, well I've been trying to take
a bit more exercise, eating better,
you know.

LAIRD
And the Lithium? How's that?

HILARY
Good.

A beat.

LAIRD
Last time you said that it made you
feel a little out of sorts?

HILARY
It's much better now. My system
must be getting used to it.

LAIRD
Really?

HILARY
Yes, much better.

(CONTINUED)

81 CONTINUED: 81

LAIRD
Excellent.

Laird scribbles in his notes. Hilary looks like someone being released from prison.

82 INT. LOCKER ROOM. DAY. 82

Close on Hilary's locker door. The sound of her footsteps as she enters the room.

Leaning up against the locker is a small brown package, obviously a 45 inch single, tied up neatly with string.

On the front of it is a deftly drawn cartoon of a Two-Tone man, with a speech bubble coming from his mouth.

It reads *"play me loud!!"*

Hilary looks down at it, delighted.

83 EXT. SHOPPING STREET/VINTAGE CLOTHES SHOP. DAY. 83

Hilary is walking down a cobbled street, filled with smaller vintage shops. She seems lighter, happy.

She stops outside a clothes shop. Looks.

84 INT. VINTAGE CLOTHES SHOP. DAY. 84

From inside the shop we see her looking through the window.

She is studying a yellow dress on a mannequin.

85 OMITTED 85

86 INT. HILARY'S FLAT. DAY. 86

Close on Hilary's hands, taking the record out of its sleeve and placing it on the turntable.

It's *Doors of Your Heart* by The Beat.

A joyous noise fills the room.

We cut back to reveal Hilary in her new yellow dress. She stands and listens. She begins to move to the rhythm, awkwardly at first, and then with increasing freedom.

(CONTINUED)

86 CONTINUED: 86

Then, all of a sudden, she is dancing with total abandon. Unselfconscious. Released.

87 EXT. MOVING COUNTRYSIDE. DAY. 87

We are moving through the softly rolling South Downs.

It's a beautiful spring day - sunny, with a gentle breeze.

88 INT. BUS. DAY. 88

The view is from the top deck of a double decker bus.

Hilary and Stephen sit next to each other. It's a classic red Thomas Tilling double-decker bus with the open rear door, ticket conductor etc.

The windows are all open, and the wind is in their hair. They are the only two people on the top deck. They are holding hands.

89 EXT. CAMBER SANDS BEACH. DUNES. DAY. 89

The two are getting changed in the dunes. Hilary - half hidden behind a sand dune - is shuffling her clothes off behind a towel. Stephen is laughing at her squirming.

STEPHEN
There's no one watching you!

HILARY
Shut up and look the other way.

STEPHEN
Why? I've seen it.

HILARY
Don't be vulgar. Anyway, it's different in the heat of passion.

STEPHEN
Well, I can't be bothered. I'm going native.

He steps out from behind the dune completely naked.

HILARY
What're you doing?!

STEPHEN
Here goes!

(CONTINUED)

89 CONTINUED: 89

And he runs off naked through the dunes, across the beach towards the sea.

STEPHEN (CONT'D)
Chaaarge!

Hilary stands there laughing, semi-clad.

As she squints after him, Stephen's figure disappears into the sun.

90 EXT. CAMBER SANDS BEACH. DUNES. EARLY AFTERNOON. 90

It is later.

We are close on Hilary as she dozes under a towel.

From off camera Stephen's hand enters frame, strokes her cheek.

She opens her eyes, looks up. Smiles.

Stephen is standing over her, grinning. He holds up two bright orange buckets and two spades.

91 EXT. CAMBER SANDS. OPEN BEACH. LATE AFTERNOON. 91

It is later still. The sun is low.

Hilary and Stephen are alone on the wide beach, completing a sand castle with the buckets and spades. The castle is big and beautiful - a large castle in the centre, surrounded by a lot of smaller towers.

Hilary is making a small tower of sand. Stephen is building a little bridge across a moat. It is nearly finished.

HILARY
How did you meet her?

STEPHEN
She was one of the nurses on my mum's ward.

HILARY
Was she the first serious girlfriend?

STEPHEN
Yeah. Broke my heart. Cried for a week.
(MORE)

(CONTINUED)

STEPHEN (CONT'D)
Still can't go near the hospital without getting butterflies.

HILARY
(cool)
Goodness.

STEPHEN
I just couldn't stop thinking about her. You know?

Hilary is silent. Is she jealous?

She makes the sand tower higher.

STEPHEN (CONT'D)
What about you?

HILARY
Oh, nothing as grand as that.

A beat.

STEPHEN
There must have been someone.

A pause. Hilary builds the tower.

STEPHEN (CONT'D)
Hilary?

HILARY
Mind your own business.

A beat. Stephen looks at her.

STEPHEN
Ok...

Stephen looks at Hilary's sand tower. It's getting higher and higher.

STEPHEN (CONT'D)
That's going to fall.

HILARY
No it isn't.

STEPHEN
And it's out of proportion with the others.

91 CONTINUED: 91

HILARY
I wasn't aware I was working under
instruction.

STEPHEN
I'm just saying.

HILARY
Well thank you. Thank you so much.

She makes the tower higher still.

STEPHEN
Why are you doing that? You're
spoiling it.

HILARY
I am not working under instruction.

STEPHEN
Alright. Do what you want.

HILARY
I shall. *Thank you.*

Beat.

HILARY (CONT'D)
(under her breath)
You men. Always have to *help* us.
Always have to *instruct* us.

STEPHEN
Don't be silly.

HILARY
You've got your hands round our
fucking necks and you won't let go.

Stephen stops working on the sandcastle.

HILARY (CONT'D)
You've got your hands round our
necks and we can't *breathe*. But you
won't let *go,* will you? You won't
fucking well let *go*.

She starts knocking down the tower.

STEPHEN
Stop. What are you doing-

91 CONTINUED: 91

HILARY
You just won't *let go*. Why don't
you just...just...

Hilary destroys the whole sand castle. It takes a while.

Stephen watches, disturbed.

She stands over it, breathless.

She looks up at Stephen, defiant.

92 INT. BUS. NIGHT. 92

They are back on the bus.

Hilary is asleep on Stephen's shoulder.

He looks down at her, puzzled, worried.

She seems small and vulnerable.

The bus stops. A MAN gets on - White, middle-aged. He sits two rows behind them.

Stephen is aware of the man's gaze. He gently adjusts Hilary's position, so she is no longer leaning on his shoulder.

Hilary remains asleep, but she is now leaning against the window. Stephen looks straight ahead.

93 EXT. BUS STOP. NIGHT. 93

Stephen and Hilary step down off the bus.

It's late and the streets are deserted.

HILARY
(warmly)
Are you going to be okay getting
home?

STEPHEN.
Sure. You?

HILARY
Oh, I'll be fine.

She walks off, turns.

(CONTINUED)

93 CONTINUED: 93

HILARY (CONT'D)
I'm in early to open up... so...
maybe see you then?

Stephen smiles. Gets it.

94 INT. ABANDONED BALLROOM. EMPIRE. MORNING. 94

Morning sunlight streams in through the huge windows.

In the furthest corner of the room, in a booth, we can see Stephen and Hilary. They are making love.

Hilary sits astride him.

Her face is turned towards the sun, her eyes closed. Lost.

95 INT. ABANDONED BALLROOM. MORNING. 95

A few minutes later. Stephen and Hilary lie on their backs. Hilary's eyes are closed. She seems happy.

Stephen's eyes are open - he stares at the ceiling.

96 INT. ABANDONED CORRIDOR. EMPIRE. MORNING. 96

Later. Hilary is creeping out of the door that leads from the ballroom, and starting to walk quietly down the corridor.

Behind her, through the crack in the door, we can see Stephen standing at the window.

97 EXT/INT. ABANDONED BALLROOM. MORNING. 97

Inside the ballroom, Stephen is looking out of the window.

Down below him, 'normal' couples walk along the front. He watches them.

98 INT. LOCKER ROOM. DAY. 98

Hilary is sitting by her locker, putting on her work shoes.

Neil quietly sits down next to her.

NEIL
(gently)
Listen Hilary, I know it's not my
business...
(MORE)

(CONTINUED)

98 CONTINUED: 98

NEIL (CONT'D)
but perhaps it might be better to
leave your personal life at home.

A beat.

HILARY
I beg your pardon?

NEIL
Rather than upstairs, in the, you
know...in the *pigeon coop.*

HILARY
(weakly)
I don't know what you mean.

Neil turns and looks at her.

NEIL
Oh, come on.

She is speechless.

NEIL (CONT'D)
(not unkindly)
Be careful, Hils. Remember what
happened before? Just...look after
yourself.

He leaves. Hilary is shaken.

99 OMITTED 99

100 OMITTED 100

101 EXT. SIDE STREET. DAY. 101

We are on the small side street that runs alongside the cinema, looking out to sea.

Hilary and Stephen come round the corner, mid-conversation. There is a distance between them.

HILARY
...I don't know how he knew, he
just did.

(CONTINUED)

STEPHEN
I think he might have seen us coming downstairs together the other day.

HILARY
It's fine. We just need to be discreet. Perhaps we should just meet outside work?

STEPHEN
Look, I think maybe it's not a good idea.

A beat.

HILARY
What do you mean?

STEPHEN
This. The whole thing.

HILARY
Why?

STEPHEN
Well...once people know, it's different.

HILARY
Really?

STEPHEN
Yes, it's just... It feels different.

A beat.

HILARY
You're embarrassed.

STEPHEN
No, I'm not. That's not what I'm saying. It's just-

HILARY
You're embarrassed, of course you are. It's silly, it's ridiculous. What are we thinking?

STEPHEN
I'm not embarrassed, I just don't-

101 CONTINUED: 101

HILARY
No. You're absolutely right. I'll see you soon.

She kisses Stephen on the cheek, and walks off, leaving him standing there.

102 INT. HILARY'S LIVING ROOM. DAY. 102

The curtains are closed in Hilary's flat.

She is sitting curled up on the floor in the corner of her living room, still in her uniform. She looks like a small animal.

She is crying.

103 INT. EMPIRE LOBBY. DAY. 103

Close on a large black and white photo in a frame. It is of The Empire in its heyday - probably around 1932. Its signage reads 'Refreshments - Wines, Spirits and Beers'. On the hoarding: *GRETA GARBO in THE PAINTED VEIL*. Well dressed crowds surround the box office.

Cutting wide, we see that the picture is leaning up against a wall in the lobby. Above it, Neil and Stephen both stand on ladders, putting up other framed and mounted photographs. They form a kind of history of the Empire over the years.

The cinema has been closed for two days while preparations take place, and it is looking pristine.

The lobby is a hive of activity. Janine, Frankie and a couple of others busy themselves around the place. Some WORKMEN are down at the front, polishing and painting the doors.

The workmen's radio in the lobby plays the news on BBC Radio 2. It is the tail end of the announcement of the engagement of Prince Charles and Lady Diana.

INTERVIEWER (ON RADIO)
...Can you take us back to when you first met?

DIANA (ON RADIO)
Yes I certainly can. It was 1977 when Charles came to stay as a friend of my sister Sarah's, for a shoot...and we sort of met in a ploughed field.

(CONTINUED)

103 CONTINUED: 103

A small chorus of 'Aaaah's from around the lobby.

NEIL
That's so sweet!

Stephen laughs incredulously.

NEIL (CONT'D)
What's the matter?

STEPHEN
What is it with you lot? You're like my mum. Why do you all care so much about a bunch of random posh people?

NEIL
What do you mean? They're the Royal Family! They make us feel good. Sane.

STEPHEN
Sane? That's a laugh. To be a Royal, you have to believe that God *put* you there in the first place, which makes you bonkers to begin with.

Neil laughs.

NEIL
Well, when you put it like that.

They carry on with their work.

104 EXT. EMPIRE. DAY. 104

Stephen sits on the steps opposite the cinema that lead down to the beach, looking out to sea. He is smoking. Behind him, workmen continue to paint the front doors of the cinema. The cinema marquee is blank.

Neil joins him, holding two mugs of tea. He hands one to Stephen.

NEIL
You heard from Hilary?

STEPHEN
No. (beat) It's been three days.

(CONTINUED)

NEIL
She told Mr Ellis she was taking
some overdue holiday. I'm sure it's
all fine.

Stephen senses there is something else. He turns and looks at Neil.

STEPHEN
So why am I worried?

A pause.

NEIL
She had a rough time last year. She
had to go away for a while in the
summer.

STEPHEN
Why?

NEIL
I think things just got a bit much
for her. Ended up being rude to a
couple of the customers, shouting
at them. She was staying longer and
longer at work, said she couldn't
sleep. Started doing weird things.

A pause.

NEIL (CONT'D)
Eventually Ellis told us she had to
go into hospital. She was away for
a few weeks, and when she came back
she was different.

STEPHEN
How?

NEIL
Just quieter. A bit sad.

STEPHEN
Did you ask her about it?

NEIL
She didn't want to talk.

Stephen takes this in.

105 INT. PROJECTION BOOTH. DAY. 105

Norman is teaching Stephen to lace up the projector.

While Stephen struggles with the cogs and sprockets, Norman smokes and holds forth. Norman wears his work coat, a brush in his top pocket.

NORMAN
In a perfect presentation the projectionist does not exist. But make no mistake, you are presenting the picture. Changing the reels, controlling the volume, all the rest. You're the last link in the chain.
(to Stephen re: the film)
Stop. Loop it.
(Stephen stares at him blankly)
Loop it under the intermittent sprocket, or it'll drag and the film will snap.

Stephen backs up, and re-threads the film more loosely.

NORMAN (CONT'D)
That's it. Now through the second fire trap...

Stephen does so. Norman continues.

NORMAN (CONT'D)
Even if it's only *one* person sitting in there, they know they aren't alone. But you don't want them to think about that. You don't want them to think about anything, really... Just watch the film.

Stephen finishes lacing the film.

STEPHEN
Done.

Norman checks Stephen's work.

NORMAN
Not bad at all.

He looks at Stephen.

NORMAN (CONT'D)
You could do this for a living.

(CONTINUED)

105 CONTINUED: 105

STEPHEN
Really?

NORMAN
Yeah, but I wouldn't recommend it.
You're far too normal.

STEPHEN
(smiling)
What do you mean?

NORMAN
Well, you know... fifteen hours a
day on your own in the dark. You
can't be a projectionist and have
any kind of actual life. I'm living
proof.

He starts to unlace the projector, and rewind the reel.

NORMAN (CONT'D)
But then, this whole place is for
people who want to escape. People
who don't belong anywhere else.
Look around you.

Stephen nods, thinks. The reel spins.

106 EXT. SEA FRONT. DAY. 106

Stephen walks along the sea front towards Hilary's building.

107 EXT. HILARY'S STREET. DAY. 107

Stephen is standing outside Paragon Apartments. He consults a small piece of paper, looks at the numbers on the buzzers.

Rings a buzzer. Looks up at the windows.

We hear distant sounds of music.

108 INT. HILARY'S APARTMENT BUILDING. DAY. 108

It is dark and smoky inside Hilary's flat.

Loud music is playing. Bob Dylan - *It's Alright Ma (I'm Only Bleeding)*.

We hear the sound of the doorbell ringing faintly, but it is drowned out by the music.

(CONTINUED)

108 CONTINUED: 108

We cut wide to reveal the state of the place. There is stuff everywhere. Clothes, overturned books, food.

On the dining table is a white notepad, dense with spidery handwriting. Next to that, a full ashtray and a half-drunk bottle of whisky. Other sheets of paper strewn about.

Hilary stands at the back window, staring out into the dusk.

She is half dressed in a bra and skirt, and is holding her blouse in her hands. She is barefoot. She has dark rings around her eyes. She appears to be in a kind of trance.

The doorbell rings again. She hears it. Turns towards the front window.

The music plays.

109 INT/EXT. HILARY'S APARTMENT BUILDING/WASTE GROUND. DAY. 109

Stephen walks out onto the waste ground in front of Hilary's building, turns and looks up at the windows.

He stops. He sees a figure walk to the window.

Hilary stares straight at him. Unreadable.

Stephen stares back at her. He is suddenly scared, although he doesn't exactly know why.

Then Hilary steps back into the shadows.

Stephen stands for a beat. Disturbed. Then he turns and starts walking back down the sea front.

110 INT. HILARY'S FLAT. DAY. 110

Inside the flat, Hilary watches Stephen walk away into the dusk. She closes the curtains.

111 EXT. EMPIRE. NIGHT. 111

A week later.

Above the awning of The Empire, it reads:

TONIGHT! - GALA PREMIERE OF *CHARIOTS OF FIRE*.

We see the Empire from a distance.

(CONTINUED)

111 CONTINUED: 111

It looks better than it has in years. Its long stretches of chrome have been polished, and it is properly lit from the outside by large arc lights. It glows brightly amongst the dark shapes of the buildings along the front.

A large, local, cheering crowd are outside. A few flashbulbs go off.

112 INT. LOBBY. NIGHT. 112

Inside, the freshly-painted lobby is heaving with people. Excited chatter, queues for popcorn. The staff - all in freshly pressed uniforms, with dickie bows etc - look after the crowd.

We observe Mr Ellis and Brenda chatting and shaking hands with local dignitaries. Jim Booth from the Mayor's office is also there.

Stephen is selling souvenir programmes, with Janine opposite him tearing tickets.

Then, a voice from the crowd.

HILARY (O.S.)
My dear young man... Don't you look absolutely *glorious*!

Stephen looks up to see Hilary. She is wearing a blue silk dress. She is heavily made up, but her hair is wild and unwashed.

There is something changed in her. A manic, dark eyed intensity. Stephen feels immediately that something is not right.

STEPHEN
Hilary! Hi!

HILARY
(loudly, to the world in general)
I know, I don't have a ticket! But that's alright, I work here. I taught him everything he knows!

She laughs loudly and moves past him.

Stephen laughs uneasily. He wants to talk to her, but the crowd is pushing forwards, and before he knows it, she is swallowed up.

(CONTINUED)

112 CONTINUED: 112

HILARY (CONT'D)
(calling to someone across
the lobby)
Hello, my darling!

As she walks away from him, Stephen can see that the zip at the back of Hilary's dress is not fully done up.

113 INT. EMPIRE SCREEN ONE. NIGHT. 113

The auditorium is full, the crowd are chatting excitedly, and holding their Gala programmes.

A microphone has been erected on stage.

There is applause as Mr Ellis walks up the small set of stairs onto the stage, and into the glare of the spotlight. He holds a small card with a list of names. He is nervous.

ELLIS
The...my Worshipful Lord Mayor and Lady Mayoress... Councillor Rushworth, Councillor Booth, my Lords, Ladies and Gentlemen, good evening. My name is Donald Ellis. I am the Manager of the Empire Cinema, perhaps the south coast's premiere film venue. It is a great honour - perhaps the greatest of my career - to welcome you to this, the regional gala premiere of *Chariots of Fire*...

Applause.

114 INT. EMPIRE SCREEN ONE. NIGHT. CONTINUOUS. 114

Ellis's address continues - a list of thank yous.

Stephen and Neil stand at the back of the auditorium, looking towards the stage. Neil leans over to whisper to Stephen.

NEIL
Where's the Mayor?

STEPHEN
There. In the middle of the front row.

He points. We see the back of the Mayor's shiny bald head, his chain glistening round his neck.

(CONTINUED)

114 CONTINUED: 114

STEPHEN (CONT'D)
Hilary's here.

NEIL
(shocked)
What? Where?

STEPHEN
Somewhere in the building.

NEIL
Is she alright?

Beat.

STEPHEN
I'm not sure.

Stephen scans the auditorium. No sign of Hilary.

115 OMITTED 115

116 INT. EMPIRE SCREEN 1. STAGE/WINGS. NIGHT. 116

On stage, Ellis is coming to the end of his speech.

ELLIS
...and so, with no further ado, I am delighted to introduce Hugh Hudson's stirring and altogether terrific... *Chariots of Fire*.

More applause.

Ellis, smiling and relieved, heads into the doorway at the bottom of the steps. As he does so, Hilary suddenly appears from the same doorway, and walks straight past a surprised Ellis towards centre stage.

The audience settle when they see her, anticipating another speech. There is a pause.

Stephen watches from the back of the auditorium with Neil.

Hilary reaches the microphone and addresses the crowd. She is clutching a folded piece of paper.

HILARY
Good evening my lords, ladies and gentlemen...Mister Mayor... My name is Hilary Small. I am Duty Manager here at the Empire, and...
(MORE)

(CONTINUED)

116 CONTINUED: 116

HILARY (CONT'D)
and as such, I thought I might add a few words of welcome.

Hilary's eyes flick to the side. We see what she sees:

Ellis is standing in the auditorium doorway, unseen by the audience. Janine stands behind him.

Ellis frantically mouths at Hilary "*What are you doing?!*"

Hilary tries to ignore him and turns to continue, her voice shaking.

HILARY (CONT'D)
Tonight is a special night. More than ever, we...we need to be... we need to feel part of a community...Black or White, it doesn't matter, it's... it's a very important... thing.

Stephen watches and holds his breath.

The microphone feeds back. Hilary looks out across the crowd. A horrible pause.

HILARY (CONT'D)
We must *celebrate*.

Nervous coughing and shuffling in the crowd.

Suddenly, Hilary remembers the piece of paper she is holding. She starts to unfold it.

HILARY (CONT'D)
So, to mark the occasion, I would like to read a poem which I think might be appropriate. It is by W.H. Auden.

She clears her throat, looks around. She reads.

HILARY (CONT'D)
"The desires of the heart are as crooked as corkscrews,
Not to be born is the best for man;
The second best is a formal order,
The dance's pattern; dance while you can."

Stephen watches, holding his breath.

116 CONTINUED: 116

HILARY (CONT'D)
(with increasing feeling)
"Dance, dance, for the figure is
easy,
The tune is catching and will not
stop;
Dance till the stars come down from
the rafters;
Dance, dance, dance till you drop."

We see Ellis in the wings. Incandescent with rage.

HILARY (CONT'D)
(to the crowd)
Thank you.

The crowd is somewhat confused, but there is a generous round of applause nonetheless.

Hilary walks into the opposite wing.

117 INT. LOBBY. NIGHT. 117

Hilary comes down the stairs into the lobby. We can hear the sound of the film starting inside Screen 1.

Ellis storms down the opposite staircase and catches up with her. A few people mill about - ushers, local press etc.

ELLIS
(a hissed whisper)
What the hell do you think you're doing? You were not invited to speak...

HILARY
Well it can't *all* be men, droning on.

Stephen comes out onto the landing and sees Hilary and Ellis talking in hushed, urgent tones. But he can't hear exactly what is being said.

ELLIS
You know how much this meant to me, Hilary. You more than anyone. And yet you *wilfully* try to ruin it.

HILARY
Well I'm terribly sorry, but you can't *always* have it your own way!

(CONTINUED)

117 CONTINUED: 117

She goes to leave. Ellis grabs her by the shoulder, spins her around.

ELLIS
You have a problem, do you know that? You need serious help. We've all tried to help you, but at some point you have to take responsibility for your own-

HILARY
(loud)
Oh, why don't you go and FUCK YOURSELF!

Suddenly everyone in the lobby falls silent.

Brenda emerges out of the auditorium onto the first floor landing, looking for Ellis.

BRENDA
Donald? What are you doing? Why aren't you inside? The film's starting.

Hilary spots her.

HILARY
Oh hello Brenda. I've been wanting to meet. I think about you *daily*.

Brenda looks at Hilary, confused.

BRENDA
I don't understand.

HILARY
Well, so many questions for a start. And so many notes to compare.

BRENDA
I'm still...unclear.

HILARY
Mostly about your husband's sexual tastes.

ELLIS
Hilary, *for God's sake*.

BRENDA
(to Hilary)
What do you mean?

(CONTINUED)

117 CONTINUED: 117

ELLIS
Brenda, this is nonsense. Please
don't listen to her.

Hilary adopts the pose of a classical actor making a speech.

HILARY
To fuck or not to fuck. That is the
question. Whether tis nobler in the
mind to wank him off into his tea
cup, or to let him fuck me over his
desk and spoil all his paperwork?

A horrible pause.

Brenda looks down at Ellis.

BRENDA
Is this true?

Ellis stands there.

BRENDA (CONT'D)
Donald. Is this true?

Suddenly Neil speaks up.

NEIL
Yes.

Neil takes a step towards Hilary, as if in solidarity.

They all look at him.

NEIL (CONT'D)
Yes, it's true.

Stephen stands half way down the stairs, dumbstruck.

Norman comes out onto the landing, unaware of what's going on.

NORMAN
(jolly)
Well, the first reel's going off
beautifully.

ELLIS
(to Hilary)
What the hell are you doing?

HILARY
Telling the truth. What a novel
idea!

(CONTINUED)

117 CONTINUED: 117

ELLIS
That's not the truth. I'll tell you the truth. You're a schizophrenic! You're a fucking *nutter*! You're only working here because I told the social workers I'd keep an eye on you. You're *unemployable*.

A pause. Hilary stands there, staring. Everyone is frozen, watching - Neil, Norman, Stephen.

Hilary turns to Brenda.

HILARY
If you want to find the condoms, they are in the top left hand drawer of his desk, next to the Murray mints.

And they all continue to watch, as Hilary turns and walks out through the front door.

118 EXT. BEACH. DAY. 118

Next day. The beach in the early morning mist.

119 EXT. SEAFRONT CAFE. DAY. 119

A cafe under one of the dilapidated colonnades on the front.

120 INT. SEAFRONT CAFE. DAY. 120

Stephen and Neil are at a table. They both nurse cups of coffee.

STEPHEN
Christ, I just... I had no idea.

NEIL
It's been going on for a while. Off and on. I caught them at it one night when they thought everyone had left. Just walked straight in on them. I think they were too busy to notice.

STEPHEN
Bloody hell. So, what are we going to do?

(CONTINUED)

120 CONTINUED: 120

NEIL
Well, Ellis says he doesn't want her back at work. Apparently she'd already threatened to smash all his windows with a golf club.

STEPHEN
(doubtful)
What? Is that really true?

NEIL
Wouldn't put it past her. He's called Social Services. They'll probably take her back into hospital.

STEPHEN
How come *he* gets away with it? It just seems so unfair.

A beat. Neil looks at him.

NEIL
Look. She's ill, Stephen. It's a serious illness. She's probably better off in St Jude's.

STEPHEN
How can she be better off in a mental hospital?

NEIL
They know how to deal with it.

Stephen shakes his head.

STEPHEN
No.

Stephen starts to get up from the table.

NEIL
What are you doing?

STEPHEN
(fishing for change in his pocket)
I'm going to see her.

NEIL
I don't think that's a good idea. I'm not sure how much help you can be.

120 CONTINUED: 120

STEPHEN
I can't just...turn my back on her.
Leave her on her own. I can't.

He puts the money on the table and leaves.

121 EXT. HILARY'S APARTMENT BUILDING. DAY. 121

Stephen is standing outside Hilary's flat, ringing on the bell again. He calls up to the window.

STEPHEN
Hilary!

No response. He rings again.

STEPHEN (CONT'D)
(shouting)
Hilary!

A buzz... the door swings slowly open.

122 INT. HILARY'S LIVING ROOM. DAY. 122

Hilary and Stephen stand facing each other in the living room. Stephen can't help but notice the chaotic state of the place.

Hilary's tone is combative.

HILARY
What do you want?

STEPHEN
I'm worried about you.

HILARY
Well that's terribly sweet, but I
don't need your concern.

STEPHEN
I thought you might want company.
Someone to talk to.

HILARY
(incredulous)
I'm absolutely *fine*! Christ, what
is *wrong* with you people?

STEPHEN
Alright, alright. But I just need
to say this.
(MORE)

(CONTINUED)

122 CONTINUED: 122

STEPHEN (CONT'D)
(beat) What you are going through is a medical condition, it's an *illness*...and, and I wanted to make sure you understand that it's not your fault.

Hilary stares at him for a moment, and then suddenly bursts out laughing.

She is doubled over, almost hysterical with laughter.

HILARY
Oh my darling Stevie! Did you take a guide book out of the library?
(she wipes her eyes)
Oh, dear...

STEPHEN
What's so funny?

HILARY
(stroking him on the cheek)
It's alright, sweetie. You don't have to try so hard.

She kisses him on the lips.

HILARY (CONT'D)
Just pour me a glass of wine.

123 INT. HILARY'S FLAT. NIGHT. 123

It's much later. Stephen and Hilary are talking.

Stephen is sat on the sofa. Hilary is manic. Energised and edgy. She paces around, smoking.

We can now see that the living room is in a much worse state than before. Tins of food are upended on the floor and table. On the wall, are various illegible scrawls, and in large letters, written in lipstick:

WOMAN = WOE-MAN

Hilary has put a couple of table lights on the floor. They cast strange shadows.

Music plays - Joni Mitchell - *'Don't Interrupt the Sorrow'*.

HILARY
I knew it as soon as my father came out of the room.
(MORE)

(CONTINUED)

123 CONTINUED: 123

HILARY (CONT'D)
I could *smell* the sex on them. Such a fucking cliche - sex with the secretary!
(she laughs mirthlessly)
I think my mother knew. She kept asking me, but I told her nothing.

STEPHEN
Why not?

HILARY
I felt loyal to him. No idea why.

She smokes.

HILARY (CONT'D)
Then she started punishing me. She blamed me for my father withdrawing his affections. I was 'Daddy's Girl'.

Pause.

HILARY (CONT'D)
When I had my first period, she brought the bedsheets to the breakfast table.

She thrusts the imaginary sheets into Stephen's face.

HILARY (CONT'D)
'Look what your precious little girl just did!'

STEPHEN
(quietly)
Jesus.

HILARY
I used to sit in the back of the car on the way to school, and I'd look at her neck...just stare at it... and I'd think, all I need to do is to put my hands round there and *squeeze*.

Stephen is watching her, frightened of her intensity.

HILARY (CONT'D)
Look at your little face! You think I'm mad, don't you? But I'm *absolutely sane*. This has all been planned. I've been lying in wait for them all this time.
(MORE)

(CONTINUED)

123 CONTINUED: 123

HILARY (CONT'D)
(escalating in intensity)
These *people*, all these *men*, they will get their comeuppance, you just *see*! *You have had your day, Mr Donald Ellis! Professor Raymond Pattenden, how DARE you give me a lower second, you corrupt little SHIT! Doctor Ian Laird, you are a fucking FRAUD! I shall report you to the highest medical authority in the LAND!*
(shaking with rage)
You're *finished!* I will *finish* you! Because I'm the *only one* who sees the truth, do you understand me?! *THE ONLY ONE!*

Suddenly, a banging on the door. They both jump.

VOICE (O.S.)
Hello? Miss Small?

They stand for a beat in silence. Then the doorbell rings.

HILARY
(to Stephen)
Turn off the music!

Stephen turns off the stereo. Hilary drops to her knees, and crawls across the floor to the light. Turns it off.

She crawls to the window. Looks out. In the darkness we can see the blue flashing lights of a police car.

HILARY (CONT'D)
Don't speak. Don't make a sound.

The sound of footsteps outside in the hallway. Then a voice through the door.

VOICE (O.S.)
Miss Small! It's Constable Bramah from Kent Police again. We have the Social Services with us. Can you let us in please?

HILARY
(to Stephen in a whisper)
Ignore them. Bastards.

Hilary and Stephen both crouch, frozen, in the near dark.

They can hear Constable Bramah's voice through the letterbox.

(CONTINUED)

123 CONTINUED: 123

BRAMAH (OS)
Miss Small, we've received further complaints from other tenants in the building about loud music and general disturbance. Also reports from Mrs Van Dyck in Flat 5 that you've made several very serious verbal and physical threats towards her.

Hilary rolls her eyes, and looks upwards towards Flat 5.

HILARY
Bitch.

BRAMAH (OS)
I'm going to need you to open this door, please!

A pause. Stephen stares at Hilary as if to say 'what do we do?'.

HILARY
Just stay quiet. They'll go away.

Then, another voice from outside.

ROSEMARY (O.S.)
Miss Small? Hilary? It's Rosemary Bates here, Kent Social Services. We've met before.

Hilary's demeanour changes the moment she hears Rosemary's voice. She stands.

ROSEMARY (CONT'D)
Hilary? Could I come in, please?

Hilary speaks to Stephen without looking at him.

HILARY
Go now. Out the back.

STEPHEN
What?

HILARY
Just leave. Use the fire escape.

STEPHEN
Why? I just want to help.

She wheels on him.

123 CONTINUED: 123

HILARY
You don't get it, do you? I don't *want* your fucking help. I'm not your patient. I'm not some problem to be solved.

ROSEMARY (O.S.)
Hilary, I'm afraid if you don't open the door, we are going to have to force entry.

HILARY
(to Stephen)
Go. *Now.*

Stephen stands frozen. Hilary stares at him.

HILARY (CONT'D)
Do I make myself clear? (beat) *Do I?*

STEPHEN
(quietly)
Yes.

HILARY
(vicious)
Good!

Stephen is stung.

HILARY (CONT'D)
(lightly)
Off you go, then.

Stephen stands to go.

BANG! Suddenly the sound of the door being battered from outside.

Stephen jumps. Hilary barely flinches.

STEPHEN
Shit!

ROSEMARY (O.S.)
Hilary? Please open the door!

BANG! Another loud bang on the door.

HILARY
(to herself)
Oh, for goodness sake...

(CONTINUED)

123 CONTINUED: 123

Hilary sighs. She suddenly seems resigned.

HILARY (CONT'D)
Just...go in there.
(she points to the next room)
And close the door.

BANG! The front door continues to be battered from the outside.

Stephen moves quickly into the next room. He turns and watches through a crack in the door.

We see Stephen's POV - Hilary walks calmly across the living room. She picks up her handbag and an overnight case.

BANG!

Hilary puts on her coat.

BANG! The door is now on its last legs.

Hilary pulls out a dining chair, so it is in the middle of the floor, and sits on it.

She looks like someone calmly waiting for a bus.

BANG! Finally the lock splinters and the door swings open.

A pause. CONSTABLE BRAMAH and ROSEMARY BATES stand on the threshold. Another POLICEMAN brings up the rear.

ROSEMARY
May we come in?

Hilary says nothing.

They enter the living room. They look around and take in the mess.

The two Policemen look to Rosemary, who takes the lead. She talks to Hilary very gently, and not unkindly, as if she is speaking to a small child.

Hilary remains sitting on the chair, very still.

ROSEMARY (CONT'D)
Hello, Hilary.

A pause. Hilary sits in silence.

(CONTINUED)

123 CONTINUED: 123

ROSEMARY (CONT'D)
It looks like things have got a little bit out of hand again? Is that right?

Still, Hilary says nothing. Rosemary sees the overnight bag.

ROSEMARY (CONT'D)
You're all packed. That's good.

Rosemary goes over to Hilary. Hilary stands.

ROSEMARY (CONT'D)
A few good days' sleep and you'll be feeling much better.

Stephen watches as they start walking towards the door.

Hilary walks upright. Trying to hold onto her dignity.

ROSEMARY (CONT'D)
We've got a first floor room all nice and ready for you.

They reach the door.

ROSEMARY (CONT'D)
This one's got a view of the garden.

They leave. The door swings closed.

Stephen steps back into the room.

He stands alone.

Fade to Black.

124 EXT. SHELTER ON SEA FRONT. DAY. 124

It is a few weeks later.

It is warmer now. The morning sun is out. People are in shirtsleeves, shorts. Kids paddle in the surf.

Stephen sits in an old victorian shelter, looking out over the beach.

He watches the people, lost in his thoughts.

125 OMITTED 125

126 INT. PROJECTION BOOTH. DAY. 126

Close on the film running through the projector.

Cut back to reveal that Stephen is in the middle of projecting a movie for the first time. He is standing next to the projector, preparing a reel change.

Norman is standing to one side, focused.

NORMAN
Listen for the reel-end bell...

Close - A small bell dings on the first projector.

NORMAN (CONT'D)
...open the dowser...

Stephen pulls a lever on the second projector.

NORMAN (CONT'D)
...here comes the first blob...

They both look out of their respective windows, waiting for the little mark in the corner of the image...

NORMAN (CONT'D)
...*motor cue*...

Stephen flicks the switch that starts the second projector.

NORMAN (CONT'D)
...here comes the second blob...

Stephen watches intently.

NORMAN (CONT'D)
...and *go*!

Stephen makes the reel change perfectly. He is pleased.

STEPHEN
Yes!

NORMAN
Excellent.
(re: the first reel)
Now get that one off and lace up reel three. Don't dick about.

126A INT. EMPIRE BOX OFFICE. DAY. (PREVIOUSLY SCENE 125) 126A

Stephen is manning the box office, selling tickets.

(CONTINUED)

126A CONTINUED: 126A

Neil steps in through the door. We can tell from his suit and his demeanour that he is now the new Manager.

NEIL
Stephen, can you do the inventory and then you can clock off early?

STEPHEN
Yeah, of course. Thanks.

127 EXT. STREETS. LATE AFTERNOON. 127

Stephen walks home up a long concrete slope. A huge grey tower block looms above him. A different kind of area to those we have seen before.

Sounds of yelling kids. A football game somewhere.

128 EXT. EXTERIOR CORRIDOR. LATE AFTERNOON. 128

Stephen walks along the outside corridor on the second floor of the flats. He gets his keys out and enters one of the doors.

129 INT. STEPHEN'S MUM'S FLAT. LATE AFTERNOON. 129

Sounds of cooking and radio in the kitchen. Stephen enters the hallway.

A Trinidadian accented voice from the kitchen.

DELIA (O.S.)
Stevie? You want Macaroni Pie?

STEPHEN
Maybe later.

He goes into his room.

130 INT. STEPHEN'S BEDROOM. LATE AFTERNOON. 130

Stephen's bedroom. The remnants of teenage years. Records, art books, an old lava lamp. Various posters. The Specials look down from the wall.

Stephen flops onto the bed.

DELIA appears in the doorway. She is a youthful mid-40s. She wears a cardigan over her nurse's uniform.

(CONTINUED)

130 CONTINUED: 130

DELIA
What's the matter?

STEPHEN
Nothing.

DELIA
What are you doing back so early?

STEPHEN
Where else am I supposed to go?

Delia sighs, and comes and sits next to him on the bed. Stephen is turned away from her.

DELIA
(gently)
Why don't you go out and have a drink?

STEPHEN
Who with?

DELIA
Well, one of your friends from the cinema or something.

Stephen laughs dismissively.

DELIA (CONT'D)
What about that girl you went to the beach with?

A pause.

DELIA (CONT'D)
Stevie?

STEPHEN
She moved away.

DELIA
Oh, that's a shame.

A beat. She strokes his back.

DELIA (CONT'D)
Well, come and have some macaroni pie. You'll feel better when you've eaten.

She leaves.

Close: The orange bucket and spade sits on the shelf.

131 INT. STEPHEN'S LIVING ROOM. NIGHT. 131

Stephen and Delia sit on the sofa, watching TV. Stephen is finishing eating the Macaroni Pie and some green beans from a plate on his lap. Delia is asleep next to him, gently snoring.

On the television, the *ITV News*.

ITV NEWS PRESENTER
...more than a hundred White and Coloured youths fought a pitched battle with the police. Some were as young as twelve, the oldest no more than twenty. It lasted for eight hours, and at the end of it, Merseyside's Chief Constable said it was a planned attack...

Stephen checks to see if his mum is sleeping. He walks over to the TV.

ITV NEWS PRESENTER (CONT'D)
...'We were set up', he said. The worst of the rioting came just after dawn-

Stephen changes the channel.

Over on BBC1, it is the game show *Blankety Blank*. The sounds of Terry Wogan and tinny laughter fill the room.

132 INT. EMPIRE LOBBY. DAY. 132

Close on Stephen's hand, as it reaches in for the box of Fruit Gums closest to the front.

Cut wide - Stephen is back at the concessions stand.

He has just finished serving someone, and is putting the money in the till...

VOICE (O.S.)
Stephen?

Stephen looks up. His expression immediately brightens.

STEPHEN
Ruby. Wow. Hi.

RUBY
(smiling)
Hi. I didn't know you worked here.

(CONTINUED)

RUBY is a striking Black woman in her early 20s.

STEPHEN
Yes. Five months now.

RUBY
I thought you wanted to go University?

STEPHEN
Yeah well, I tried. Still trying.

RUBY
I'm not at the Hospital anymore. Your mum probably told you.

STEPHEN
No, she didn't say anything.

RUBY
It was the hours, those early mornings. I don't know how they do it.

STEPHEN
(laughing awkwardly)
Right, I know. So... what do you do now?

RUBY
Well, for the time being I'm working at that bar on the front. Boodles. It's fun. You should pop in, maybe have a drink.

STEPHEN
Yeah. Might do that.

They look at each other for a beat.

RUBY
And in the meantime, a box of Maltesers, please.

STEPHEN
Oh right, yes, of course.

She puts the money on the counter.

STEPHEN (CONT'D)
Enjoy *Stir Crazy*. It's excellent.

He hands her the chocolates.

132 CONTINUED: 132

RUBY
Thanks... See you soon, then?

STEPHEN
Yeah. See you soon.

Ruby smiles and walks off. Stephen tries to hide his delight.

132A EXT. CRAZY GOLF. DAY. 132A

Plastic seagulls. Dwarf palm trees. A small windmill.

Stephen and Ruby are playing mini-golf. Ruby sinks an unlikely putt. Stephen laughs and cheers. They kiss.

133 OMITTED 133

134 EXT. SEA FRONT. DAY. 134

It's dusk. The two of them walk back along the front. Ruby is eating an ice cream.

They are holding hands.

STEPHEN
...I don't know. Maybe stay on
here, keep working at the Empire.
Help Norman out.

RUBY
Who?

STEPHEN (V.O.)
The projectionist. He's funny. I
like it up there. Once you get over
the smell.

RUBY
(laughing)
Yeah, that's cool. All those movies
for free.

STEPHEN
Well, you don't really get to watch
any of them...

Stephen spots something up ahead. Slows down.

(CONTINUED)

134 CONTINUED: 134

Ahead of him he sees Hilary. She is sat alone on a bench, with a shopping bag next to her. She has a hat pulled down low.

She looks ten years older than when we last saw her. Her hair has grown longer, and she wears no make-up.

She is staring out to sea.

RUBY
What is it?

STEPHEN
Nothing. Someone I know.

RUBY
Do you want to say hello?

STEPHEN
Nah. It's fine.

They keep walking past Hilary on the bench. She doesn't see them.

As they pass, Stephen looks down at Hilary. Small wisps of grey hair peek out from underneath Hilary's hat.

They walk on a moment in silence. Stephen is thinking.

RUBY
You ok?

Stephen remains lost in thought.

RUBY (CONT'D)
Stevie?

STEPHEN
What? (beat) Yeah. I'm fine.

They walk a bit more.

STEPHEN (CONT'D)
You know what? I feel a bit...

He stops. Ruby looks at him.

STEPHEN (CONT'D)
I think I should go back and say hello. Do you mind waiting here for a sec?

134 CONTINUED: 134

RUBY
(slightly confused)
Oh... okay.

STEPHEN
I won't be long.

He turns and jogs back along the front.

135 OMITTED 135

136 EXT. SEA FRONT. DAY. 136

We are with Hilary as she looks out across the beach.

STEPHEN (O.S.)
Hilary.

Hilary turns and sees Stephen.

HILARY
Hello. How are you?

She speaks to Stephen as if she barely knows him.

Stephen doesn't know this, but she is heavily medicated, and only just out of the Psychiatric Unit.

STEPHEN
I'm good.

An awkward pause.

STEPHEN (CONT'D)
So, you're back.

HILARY
Yes. (beat) Out and about again.

STEPHEN
Great. It's good to see you. We miss you.

HILARY
(a little laugh)
I'm sure that's not true.

STEPHEN
Why don't you drop by? Say hello to everyone. (beat) You know, Ellis has left. Moved to Broadstairs.

(CONTINUED)

136 CONTINUED: 136

HILARY
Yes, Neil told me. (beat) He called me and asked me back.

She looks up at him to see his response.

STEPHEN
Wow. That's brilliant.

Ruby has walked up behind Stephen, curious. She is still holding her ice cream.

Hilary spots her over Stephen's shoulder.

HILARY
(not unfriendly)
Hello.

RUBY
Hi.

STEPHEN
This is Ruby. Ruby, this is Hilary. Who I know from work.

Hilary smiles at Ruby. Another awkward pause.

STEPHEN (CONT'D)
Ok, so... hopefully see you soon.

HILARY
Yes.

They leave.

Hilary stays sitting on the bench.

137 INT/EXT. EMPIRE. DAY. 137

A few days later.

Close on the last letter 'L' being secured into position on the awning.

Cut wide to reveal the front of the Empire.

Janine is climbing down a ladder at the front of the cinema, having just changed the movie titles for the week.

They now read:

SCREEN 1 - *PRIVATE BENJAMIN* SCREEN 2 - *RAGING BULL*

138 INT. EMPIRE. DAY. 138

Janine walks back inside the lobby.

Stephen is working at the concessions stand. He serves a customer. He looks up.

Opposite him, Hilary is now taking tickets. She is no longer dressed in the Duty Manager's waistcoat.

Stephen watches her. She doesn't look over to him.

Hilary takes the final ticket. She looks around unsure what to do next. Lost.

Stephen watches her, concerned.

139 INT. LOBBY LANDING. DAY. 139

Hilary is sitting on a bench looking out over the empty lobby. Her uneaten lunch next to her. She seems very downcast.

STEPHEN (O.C.)
Hilary?

She stares straight ahead.

STEPHEN (CONT'D)
Hilary? Are you alright?

Hilary looks up at Stephen. He is standing next to her.

HILARY
(quietly)
Stephen. Tell me truthfully. Did I humiliate myself?

STEPHEN
What?

Hilary looks at Stephen. Her eyes are filled with tears.

HILARY
Did I? Tell me.

Stephen sits down next to her. A pause.

STEPHEN
No. It wasn't humiliating. It was just...intense.

A pause.

(CONTINUED)

139 CONTINUED: 139

STEPHEN (CONT'D)
I thought you were a bit of a hero
to be honest.

She smiles weakly.

HILARY
That's nice of you.

She continues to stare out over the lobby towards the sea.

HILARY (CONT'D)
But it's hard to believe.

After a moment.

HILARY (CONT'D)
My dad used to take me fishing when
I was little. I think he wished I
was a boy. (beat) We never caught
anything, and for years I thought
he was a bad fisherman. But then I
realised it was something else,
something quite simple. He didn't
know where the fish were, and he
was ashamed to ask. (beat) He was
just...ashamed.

A beat. She looks at him.

HILARY (CONT'D)
Shame is not a healthy condition.

A pause.

STEPHEN
You should try and forget about it.
(beat) Go in there more often.

He indicates the auditorium.

HILARY
No. I can't. It's my job.

STEPHEN
You take the tickets, you make sure
they're all in their seats, but you
never go in. You should watch once
in a while.
(with feeling)
(MORE)

(CONTINUED)

139 CONTINUED: 139

STEPHEN (CONT'D)
Sit in the middle of a bunch of people who don't know you, who've never met you, who can't even *see* you. (beat) That little beam of light is escape.

She looks at him. The light in his eyes.

HILARY
I missed you.

Stephen smiles.

STEPHEN
Come on. We've got a little surprise for you.

140 INT. LOCKER ROOM. DAY. 140

Hilary walks in.

There is a big cheer as she enters.

The whole staff have gathered to welcome her back.

A homemade banner has been stretched across the room. It reads "WELCOME BACK HILARY". There are a few balloons. Someone chucks a handful of coloured confetti.

Hilary covers her mouth in shock and surprise. She is genuinely touched.

NEIL
Thank God you're here, I need some of that cake!

Laughter. Janine brings a chocolate cake out of her locker with a single candle in it.

JANINE
(re: the cake)
Ta-daa! Safeway's finest!

Another cheer.

141 INT. LOCKER ROOM. DAY. 141

It is a little later. Everyone sits round chatting, eating cake, talking over each other. Janine has put some music on a boombox in the corner - Joy Division's *Transmission*.

Hilary sits in the middle of it all, enjoying the hubbub.

(CONTINUED)

141 CONTINUED: 141

Then she hears something. Neil does too.

NEIL
Wait - can you hear that? What's that noise?

They all gradually go quiet and listen.

Someone turns the music down.

In the distance, we can hear the sound of hundreds of engines getting closer.

142 INT. LOBBY. DAY. 142

The staff all come out of the locker room into the lobby to see what's going on. Norman has come down the stairs from the projection booth and is standing in the lobby.

NORMAN
Motorbikes.

A procession of scooters is already in progress along the front - straight past the front window of the cinema.

They all gather to watch, as - one by one - a mass of Vespas, Lambrettas and Piaggios pass by the front window.

The light catches their gleaming chrome. It is an amazing sight.

JANINE
Wow. Look at that.

The bikes are all festooned and adorned with mirrors. The riders are Mods - they wear Parkas, drainpipe trousers, badges, bowling shoes.

The staff all watch, mesmerised, as the procession of scooters goes past.

Then, above the sound of the bikes, and getting closer, horns, Klaxons, and in the distance, chanting.

The staff all watch as the energy outside begins to change. Angrier now.

Following the motorbike riders are people on foot. Skinheads, although not all of them. British Movement tattoos and Harringtons; Doc Marten boots and braces. There are a few National Front banners being held aloft, and a couple of swastikas.

(CONTINUED)

142 CONTINUED: 142

The atmosphere outside suddenly feels very ugly.

Norman turns to Neil.

NORMAN
I think you'd better lock the door.

Neil moves towards the door.

NEIL
Stephen, quick, give me a hand.

Stephen hurries to the front doors. He and Neil lock them.

Then, outside, a couple of the marchers spot Stephen.

They shout to each other, their voices muffled by the glass.

SKINHEADS
Fuck me, look at this! There's a fucking coon in here!

They shout to each other.

SKINHEADS (CONT'D)
Oi! Over here!

Several stop and turn and come to the windows, holding their hands up to their eyes to see inside.

COLIN, the skinhead who we met in the street earlier, walks up to the window and looks inside. He sees Stephen, and starts to rhythmically bang on the window.

Stephen starts backing away into the shadows. The other staff don't know what to do.

STEPHEN
(quietly to himself)
Shit.

Suddenly there are a lot of faces staring at them through the glass, yelling. Perhaps thirty or forty, silhouetted, cutting out the light.

Now they all start banging on the windows. The noise is deafening.

NEIL
Hilary! Call the police!

Hilary is frozen. She doesn't want to abandon Stephen.

NB - we see most of what follows from Hilary's point of view.

(CONTINUED)

142 CONTINUED: 142

The pounding on the windows and doors gets still louder. The whole building is shaking.

NEIL (CONT'D)
What the hell are you doing? For Christ's sake, someone call the police!

CRASH! One of the large windows caves in. One of the skinheads has cut his hand on the glass.

SKINHEAD
Aaargh! Fucking *shit*!

There is blood all over his hand.

CRASH! Someone has kicked a door in.

Then everything happens very fast.

Rioters are yelling and coming in through the doors.

Skinheads and rioters are inside the lobby.

Hilary is screaming at Stephen to run. Others are shouting.

Stephen tries to escape towards the locker room. Hilary watches as Colin and two other skinheads catch him, and drag him back into the middle of the lobby.

STEPHEN
Don't fucking touch me!

Rioters are ransacking the concessions stand, nicking sweets. Some of them are kids.

The sound of more glass shattering, people have broken into the box office, trying to open the till.

They are backing Stephen up against the wall. He beckons them on, eyes wide.

STEPHEN (CONT'D)
Alright, come on then, you bunch of fucking cowards.

COLIN
(walking towards Stephen)
What did you say?

MIKEY
...leave him Col. Just leave it.

COLIN
I'm not a fucking coward, you fucking spade.

Stephen's eyes are wide with fury. A circle of jeering skinheads surrounds him now. They are egging Colin on...

STEPHEN
Yeah? Why d'you bring all your friends then? Can't do anything on your own? Get some imagination, you fucking coward.

With that, Colin launches himself at Stephen. A couple of skinheads join him, others scream abuse. Mikey is shouting at Colin to stop and trying to grab him. It is chaos.

Stephen tries to land some punches. He is kicked to the ground. Kicks and punches rain down.

Through the group of rioters, Hilary can see Stephen silently staring up at them. Defiant.

Norman has come out of the back room and is yelling to everyone that he's called the police.

In the middle of all the chaos Pogo has jumped up on the concessions stand, and is dancing alone to the music in his head.

Neil has an office chair up in front of him, and is trying to push the rioters back out again. A rioter grabs the chair, pushes Neil to the ground.

Hilary is still shouting, trying to fight her way to Stephen.

HILARY
Stop! Stop! Leave him alone!

Stephen is now being savagely beaten by three or four skinheads. He drops into a foetal position, hidden behind a crowd of rioters. Hilary loses sight of him. She is frantic.

Then suddenly the sound of Police sirens. People start to scatter. Some rioters start to run towards the doors.

Hilary desperately pushes people aside to get to Stephen.

Colin has completely lost control and is repeatedly kicking Stephen in the stomach. Hilary flings herself on him, grabbing his arms and trying to drag him off.

Colin wrestles with Hilary. He throws her off him. Hilary falls to the ground, winded.

(CONTINUED)

142 CONTINUED: 142

Several Police cars pull up outside the doors, their sirens very loud. Some police come into the lobby, and try to tackle the last few rioters.

Colin tries to make a run for it, but is tackled by two policemen.

The rioters have scattered. Several policemen have now jumped out of their cars and are chasing the rest of the rioters back along the front.

Hilary catches her breath, pulls herself up and walks over to Stephen. She stops, looks down.

Stephen lies semi-conscious, a pool of blood around his head and face.

143 INT. AMBULANCE. DAY. 143

Hilary sits next to Stephen, who is semi-conscious on a gurney. He is hooked up to an oxygen machine and heart monitor.

Hilary holds his hand. She is white with fear.

144 EXT. AMBULANCE. DAY. 144

We are with the ambulance as it races through the streets.

145 INT. AMBULANCE. DAY. 145

Hilary looks down.

Stephen is breathing fast. He opens his eyes, staring upwards. His face is slick with blood. There are angry cuts around his cheek and mouth, his lips are swollen. One eye has closed up completely.

HILARY
You're going to be alright. You're strong.

He slowly turns to look at her. His hand closes around hers.

146 EXT/INT. HOSPITAL A&E. ENTRANCE. DAY. 146

Stephen is now unconscious. He has an airway in his mouth and is connected to an oxygen tank. He is being pushed on the gurney towards the doors of the Queen Elizabeth Hospital.

(CONTINUED)

146 CONTINUED: 146

Hilary has climbed down from the ambulance, and is following the PARAMEDICS.

An atmosphere of intense focus and suppressed panic.

147 INT. HOSPITAL A&E. LOBBY. DAY. 147

The Paramedics push their way into the crowded lobby. Hilary follows.

PARAMEDIC
Coming through!

They are met by the RECEIVING DOCTOR and NURSE, also on the move.

PARAMEDIC (CONT'D)
He's had a kicking. GCS dropped to 6, and he just lost consciousness.

DOCTOR
(moving people aside)
Coming through! Excuse me please!

PARAMEDIC
Respirations thirty five per minute.

DOCTOR
Move please!

They push the gurney through the swing doors and disappear. The Nurse turns to Hilary.

NURSE
Are you next of kin?

HILARY
I...no, I'm a friend, I work with him.

NURSE
Next of kin only past this point.

HILARY
But I'm... will he be alright?

But the Nurse is already moving off.

NURSE
If you want to wait here, we'll let you know.

(CONTINUED)

147 CONTINUED: 147

And she's gone, through the swing doors.

Hilary stands, watching her go.

148 EXT/INT. HOSPITAL A&E, WAITING AREA. NIGHT. 148

It's several hours later. The place is much emptier.

From outside, through the windows, we can see Hilary sitting alone on a chair, under the fluorescent lights.

149 INT. HOSPITAL A&E, WAITING AREA. NIGHT. 149

Later still. Hilary is filling a plastic cup of tea from a dispensing machine. She is still shaky.

VOICE (O.S.)
Are you waiting for news of Stephen?

Hilary turns.

It's Stephen's mum, Delia, in her nurse's uniform.

HILARY
Yes.

DELIA
He's going to be alright.

HILARY
(closing her eyes with relief)
Oh, thank God.

DELIA
Badly bruised all over. Lost a couple of teeth. But he's conscious, and he wanted you to know he was ok.

HILARY
Oh, that's... *Thank you.*

Hilary looks at Delia.

HILARY (CONT'D)
I'm so sorry.

Delia nods.

(CONTINUED)

149 CONTINUED: 149

DELIA
Yes. It's a bad situation.

Delia looks at Hilary. A pause. There is some slight suspicion in her manner.

DELIA (CONT'D)
Anyway. You can go home now. You must have been here for hours.

HILARY
Ok...yes. I'll just get my stuff.

Hilary turns and heads across the waiting area.

Then, from across the room:

DELIA
Were you the one he went to the beach with?

It takes Hilary a moment. She turns.

HILARY
Oh, yes. Yes, we did go to the beach.

Delia nods. Looks at Hilary. There is something in Delia's eyes. Disappointment?

Then Delia turns and leaves.

150 INT. HILARY'S BATHROOM. NIGHT. 150

Hilary stands under the shower, eyes closed.

She looks down at her hand. Stephen's blood is still on it. She washes it off.

151 INT. HILARY'S LIVING ROOM. NIGHT. 151

Hilary sits on the sofa, dressed in her dressing gown. We can see that her knees are bruised and grazed from the scuffle. She holds a glass of whisky, untouched.

She is staring blankly at the television. It is now past midnight.

The screen has shifted to the BBC1 Clock.

151 CONTINUED: 151

BBC ANNOUNCER
Well, now the time is almost six and a half minutes past twelve, and BBC One is closing down. So, from all of us here, this is Henry Brooks wishing you a very good night.

The National Anthem plays.

152 EXT. SEAFRONT. DAY. 152

It is pouring with rain.

People hide in shopfronts away from the downpour.

Hilary hurries along the seafront under an umbrella.

153 INT. EMPIRE LOBBY. DAY. 153

Through the smashed and boarded up front windows of the cinema we can see the rain pouring down.

A few audience members are leaving a screening. Otherwise, the lobby is very quiet and almost empty. There is a strange suppressed atmosphere.

Hilary stands behind the concessions stand, detached, as if in a dream.

154 EXT. HOSPITAL. DAY. 154

Still raining.

A figure stands outside the Hospital under an umbrella, holding a bunch of flowers.

It is Hilary. She is hesitating, not sure whether to go in.

She loses her nerve. She turns away.

155 EXT. SIDE STREETS. NIGHT. 155

The rain has stopped, but the cobbles are still wet. The streets are mostly empty.

Neil and Hilary are walking home through small side streets.

(CONTINUED)

155 CONTINUED: 155

NEIL
I like it when it's been raining
and there's no one around.

HILARY
Yes.

NEIL
I love it here.

HILARY
Mmm.

They walk a bit in silence.

NEIL
You seem much better, Hilary. Have
you seen the doctor again?

HILARY
A different one, yes. I think I
burned my bridges with the last
chap.

She laughs gently.

NEIL
(slightly sheepish)
Did he give you some, you know...
some stuff to take.

HILARY
Yes. Not the old stuff. That was
like being on the moon.

Neil laughs.

HILARY (CONT'D)
This stuff seems better.

NEIL
Thats great, Hilary. *Really*. Well
done.

Hilary looks at him. Smiles.

HILARY
Well, we'll see... But, thank you.
And thanks for my job back. It
means a lot.

NEIL
And I'm always around if you need
someone to talk to.

(CONTINUED)

155 CONTINUED: 155

Hilary nods, and looks away. She is thinking of Stephen.

They are approaching a pub. Neil stops outside it, points.

NEIL (CONT'D)
Quick one?

HILARY
Lethal cocktail of alcohol and
psychotropic drugs... Why not?

Neil smiles. They head into the pub.

156 EXT. EMPIRE FIRE ESCAPE. LATE AFTERNOON. 156

A few days later. The sun is low over the sea.

It is late afternoon, end of a hot day.

Hilary sits outside, on the fire escape. She is perched on the stairs, with her money box and clipboard, checking last night's ticket stubs.

Norman is walking down the fire escape, loading the last of a set of film canisters onto a hand cart. He trudges back up the steps, out of breath.

NORMAN
(walking up the steps)
I have to say, I miss our young
friend. I was getting used to
someone helping me with all this.

Hilary doesn't look up.

HILARY
Mm.

Norman continues his journey.

NORMAN
You been to visit him?

HILARY
A couple of weeks ago.

NORMAN
Not since?

A beat. Norman stops next to her.

HILARY
No.

(CONTINUED)

156 CONTINUED: 156

NORMAN
Go and see him then. Don't run away.

Hilary looks up at him.

HILARY
Is that what I'm doing?

NORMAN
Seems like it.

He sits down next to her, takes out a tin of rolled up cigarettes. Offers one to Hilary. She takes it.

NORMAN (CONT'D)
What are you frightened of, Hilary?

Hilary silently asks herself the question.

HILARY
I'm not sure.

Norman lights her cigarette, then his. Exhales.

NORMAN
(matter of fact)
I've got a son. Christopher. He's twenty-two now. Lives in London. Haven't seen him since he was eight.

Hilary is amazed.

HILARY
What?

NORMAN
He doesn't want to see me and I don't blame him. (beat) Basically, I ran away.

HILARY
Why?

NORMAN
What?

HILARY
Why?

A pause. He thinks.

(CONTINUED)

156 CONTINUED: 156

NORMAN
(with deep sadness)
I can't remember.

He stares out, tears in his eyes.

157 INT. HILARY'S LIVING ROOM. NIGHT. 157

It is the evening. Hilary stands putting on her coat.

She checks herself in the mirror. Steels herself.

158 INT. HOSPITAL CORRIDOR/NURSE'S STATION. NIGHT. 158

Hilary walks up to the nurse's station and asks the way to the ward. The NURSE points the way.

Hilary holds a small yellow plastic bag.

159 INT. HOSPITAL WARD. NIGHT. 159

A crowded, messy hospital ward. Hilary stands for a moment, looking for Stephen. Nervous.

Then Hilary spots him in a bed at the far end of the ward.

Stephen looks up and sees her. He smiles.

160 INT. HOSPITAL WARD. NIGHT. 160

Hilary is sitting at Stephen's bedside.

STEPHEN
...a couple of cracked ribs, so it's a bit sore when I laugh. But the swelling's gone down, and my eyesight's ok, so...

A pause.

HILARY
I'm so sorry, Stephen. I don't know what to say.

STEPHEN
There's nothing to say. It happened to my mum, it's happened to me, it'll probably happen to my children. Sometimes I think, what's the fucking point?

(CONTINUED)

She has no answer. They sit for a moment.

HILARY
Here. I've got something for you.

She reaches down, lifts up the yellow plastic bag. It's from Bionic Records. She pulls out a new LP - *'W'Happen?'* by *The Beat.*

HILARY (CONT'D)
Just came out. Thought you might like it.

STEPHEN
(surprised)
Oh my God!

He looks at the album, its joyful multicoloured sleeve, turning it over in his hand.

STEPHEN (CONT'D)
That's so nice of you.

HILARY
The chap in the shop gave me a bit of an odd look. But then I suppose I don't much look like a "Rude Girl".

She says it with heavy inverted commas. Stephen laughs. He pulls out the inner sleeve of the LP, looking at the lyrics and the photos of the band.

HILARY (CONT'D)
(looking at the LP too)
I didn't really get what was so special about it all before. But I can see now, it's a kind of Utopia.

STEPHEN
What?

HILARY
Black kids and White kids meeting up together.
(gesturing to the record)
This just makes it...normal.

STEPHEN
Yeah.

He looks at Hilary.

160 CONTINUED: 160

STEPHEN (CONT'D)
Good music, too.

She smiles. A voice from behind her.

DELIA
Hello.

Hilary turns and sees Delia. She reflexively stands up.

DELIA (CONT'D)
It's okay, you don't need to leave,
I'm just doing last check-ups.

HILARY
(slightly flustered)
No, I should go... I've got stuff I
need to do, and it's late and I
don't want to be a bother.

She gathers her stuff.

HILARY (CONT'D)
(to Stephen)
Bye, then.

STEPHEN
Bye Hilary. Thanks for coming.

She bends to give him a kiss on the cheek. They are both very aware of Delia's presence. It is awkward.

HILARY
Bye.

She leaves.

161 INT. HOSPITAL CORRIDOR. EVENING. 161

Hilary walks away down the corridor.

After a moment, Delia appears behind her, at the other end of the corridor.

DELIA
(calling out)
Hilary!

Hilary stops and turns. Delia walks up to her.

(CONTINUED)

161 CONTINUED: 161

DELIA (CONT'D)
Look...Hilary. I don't know what's gone on between you two, and I don't really want to, but you should know that he was asking after you. He likes you. You cheer him up. So... thank you.

She reaches out and squeezes Hilary's hand. Then she turns and leaves.

We see Hilary's face. Her eyes are filled with tears.

162 EXT. STREET OUTSIDE HOSPITAL. NIGHT. 162

Hilary comes running out of the Hospital.

She runs along the cab rank to the front. Climbs into the cab.

163 INT. CAB. NIGHT. 163

Hilary speaks to the driver.

HILARY
Empire Cinema on the front, please.

164 EXT. SEAFRONT/EMPIRE. NIGHT. 164

It's late at night. The seafront is mostly empty.

We see the front of the Empire. This week's movies:

SCREEN 1 - *BEING THERE* SCREEN 2 - *GREGORY'S GIRL*

The entryway lights and the lights in the lobby have been turned off for the night.

The cab pulls up outside. We see Hilary getting out, hurrying to the front doors.

165 INT. LOBBY. NIGHT. 165

Norman has come out of the projection room and is coming down the stairs, dressed in his coat and hat. He is holding the keys, about to lock up and leave for the night.

He stops.

165 CONTINUED: 165

Hilary is standing in the centre of the lobby, in the near darkness, out of breath.

HILARY
Show me a film.

Norman stares at her for a moment.

NORMAN
What?

HILARY
Show me a film. (beat) I want to see a film.

Norman gets it.

NORMAN
What film?

HILARY
Any film. You choose.

He smiles and nods.

166 INT. CORRIDOR/INT. EMPIRE SCREEN ONE. NIGHT. 166

Hilary walks down the darkened corridor towards Screen 1.

The auditorium is silent and empty as Hilary steps in.

We watch her walk down a row of seats, take off her coat and sit in the centre of the row.

The curtains slowly open.

167 INT. PROJECTION BOOTH. NIGHT. 167

Inside the booth, Norman meticulously threads the film through the projector.

He flicks a switch. In close up we see the carbons ignite.

The projector whirrs into life.

168 INT. EMPIRE SCREEN ONE. NIGHT. 168

A moment of darkness and the film begins. It is Hal Ashby's *Being There*. But we don't see much of it. We remain mostly with Hilary.

(CONTINUED)

168 CONTINUED: 168

On screen Chance the Gardener (Peter Sellers) is waking up.

We slowly push in on Hilary's face as she descends into the world of the film. Instantly immersed.

169 INT. PROJECTION BOOTH. NIGHT. 169

Inside the booth, the silence is only broken by the whirring of the shutter, and the hum of the film running through the projector.

We see the photo of the little boy on the wall. Norman's son.

Norman looks out of the small projection booth window.

We see what he sees: Hilary, a tiny figure in the auditorium, sitting alone, the beam of light slicing through the dark.

170 INT. EMPIRE SCREEN ONE. NIGHT. 170

We see Hilary's face, utterly rapt.

We push in closer.

170A INT. PROJECTION BOOTH. NIGHT. 170A

Norman does a reel change, concentrating intently.

170B INT. EMPIRE SCREEN 1. NIGHT. 170B

We push in on Hilary. Closer still.

171 INT. PROJECTION BOOTH. NIGHT. 171

Inside the booth, Norman rewinds a reel.

As he does so, we slowly pull back to reveal all the photos on the wall.

All those faces looking out at us.

All those movies.

172 INT. EMPIRE SCREEN ONE. EVENING. 172

On screen, we have reached the end of the movie.

(CONTINUED)

172 CONTINUED: 172

Hilary watches as - very slowly - Chance the Gardener walks across the water to the music of Erik Satie.

We are very close on Hilary.

She is frozen, as she watches the final line of the film.

MELVYN DOUGLAS (O.C.)
Life...is a state of mind.

And the movie cuts to black.

It is dark, but there is enough light to see the tears rolling down Hilary's face.

It's as if the floodgates have opened. She has finally let go.

She doesn't bother to wipe the tears away.

173 INT. PROJECTION BOOTH. NIGHT. 173

Inside the projection booth, Norman carefully places a film reel back in its canister.

He walks to the door, switches off the lights.

The door closes. Darkness.

174 EXT/INT. CAFE. DAY. 174

A little hexagonal cafe on the beach.

Inside, morning sunlight streaks through the windows.

Stephen and Hilary are sitting having breakfast.

Stephen is looking much better. His facial bruising has all but disappeared. He suddenly feels older. A man.

Hilary is animated. Stephen is listening, but preoccupied.

HILARY
It was just...wonderful. I can't wait to see it again.

STEPHEN
Yeah. Peter Sellers is the funniest. You should see him in *Return of the Pink Panther*.
(imitating Inspector Clouseau's french accent)
(MORE)

174 CONTINUED: 174

STEPHEN (CONT'D)
'I did not know the bank was being *robed*'. Hilarious.

HILARY
I can't wait. And there are so many others! You're going to need to make me a list.

STEPHEN
Of course. Look-

HILARY
I was thinking maybe it could be a weekly thing. You know - midnight screenings. I'm sure we could persuade Norman-

STEPHEN
(Interrupting)
I've got a place at college. (Beat). I'm going to college.

Hilary is totally blindsided, but she does a good job of hiding it.

STEPHEN (CONT'D)
I got a letter two weeks ago. A place opened up.

HILARY
Stephen that's...that's wonderful. Where?

STEPHEN
Bristol. (beat) Architecture.

Hilary looks at him.

HILARY
You did it.

Stephen nods.

STEPHEN
You told me not to give up.

She manages a smile.

HILARY
Congratulations, Stephen. You deserve it.

They sit for a moment drinking their tea. There is suddenly nothing to say. Then Hilary realises something.

(CONTINUED)

174 CONTINUED: 174

HILARY (CONT'D)
When are you leaving?

A beat.

STEPHEN
Tomorrow.

Hilary is shocked.

175 EXT. STEPHEN'S FLAT. DAY. 175

Stephen walks along the outside corridor of his block of flats, lets himself into the front door. He has a few shopping bags with him - new stuff for college.

175A INT. STEPHEN'S FLAT. DAY. 175A

As he enters, Delia appears from the kitchen.

DELIA
What did you get?

STEPHEN
New shoes. And those books for the course.

DELIA
That's great. (beat) Did you tell her?

STEPHEN
Yes.

DELIA
Was she ok?

STEPHEN
Yes. (beat) No. (beat) I don't know.

Delia comes over to him.

DELIA
Well. As long as you were kind.

He nods. She strokes his face.

DELIA (CONT'D)
Now. Ruby's coming over for your goodbye dinner, so what we gonna make her?

176 INT. LIVING ROOM/KITCHEN. NIGHT. 176

It's later.

We see the three of them - Stephen, Delia and Ruby - through the open door to the kitchen. The remains of supper is on the table. A bottle of wine has been opened.

They are laughing. Stephen dings his glass, and stands to make a toast.

DELIA
Don't break the glass, Stevie, those are the good ones!

STEPHEN
Alright Mum, calm down, I'll be gone tomorrow.

They laugh. He raises his glass.

STEPHEN (CONT'D)
So. (A pause) Here's to the future...and to good music...and to getting back up. (beat) And here's to Richard Pryor and John Belushi...and Mars Bars...and sand castles...and my new suede shoes.

He pauses, and looks at the two women at the table, both looking back at him with love.

STEPHEN (CONT'D)
And here's to going away. (beat) And coming home.

Delia and Ruby applaud and cheer.

STEPHEN (CONT'D)
And now...I need to pee.

He heads to the toilet. A pause while they watch him go.

RUBY
God, Mrs Murray. He's so different from before.

Delia nods.

DELIA
Lived a little bit of life, I think.

She looks after him.

DELIA (CONT'D)
A little bit of life.

177 EXT. PARK. DAY. 177

It is a glorious morning.

Stephen walks through an avenue of trees in the park. He has his large duffel bag over his shoulder.

Morning light rakes through the trees and dapples the ground.

There is a lightness to his step. He is off to college.

He looks. Up ahead, waiting for him on a bench, sits Hilary.

She sees him and smiles.

178 EXT. PARK. DAY. 178

Close on a small paper bag with a book inside it. Hilary hands it to Stephen.

HILARY
Read it later.

Stephen takes it.

STEPHEN
Thanks, Hilary.

They sit together on the bench, looking out across the park, unsure of what to say.

HILARY
You'll have a wonderful time. But I'm going to miss you.

STEPHEN
Yeah, I'll miss you too. (beat) Any sage advice?

HILARY
(smiling)
What, from the old-timer? No, not really.

STEPHEN
Nothing? Not even with all your posh university experience?

She thinks.

178 CONTINUED: 178

HILARY
You can only play the hand you're dealt.

A beat.

STEPHEN
What does that mean?

HILARY
It means... don't hope for too much.

STEPHEN
(genuinely puzzled)
Why? (beat) Isn't it better to hope for everything?

HILARY
Maybe.

STEPHEN
Better to try, at least. Shoot for the moon. Otherwise, why do it?

A beat. She looks at Stephen.

HILARY
Yes. You're right. Ignore me. Silly, depressing woman.

Hilary stands.

HILARY (CONT'D)
Alright. Off you go.

STEPHEN
Ok.

She can't meet his eye.

STEPHEN (CONT'D)
See you in the holidays maybe?

HILARY
Yes. That would be lovely.

STEPHEN
Ok. Bye.

And he turns and leaves.

She lifts her head to watch him go.

179 EXT. PARK. DAY. 179

We are with Stephen as he walks away, shouldering his bag.

Then, from behind him, we hear Hilary's voice.

HILARY (O.S.)
Stephen!

He turns, and she's in his arms.

They hold each other. She is clinging onto him. He hugs her fiercely too, head buried in her hair.

They stand there, holding each other.

A few people turn their heads as they pass, staring at the strange sight of a middle aged White woman and a young Black man standing, hugging, in the park.

180 EXT. RAILWAY STATION. DAY. 180

Stephen stands under the wrought iron canopy of the railway station.

He is looking up at the wooden departure board. The clickety-clack of the red and white flap indicators announces his train.

181 INT. TRAIN CARRIAGE. DAY. 181

Stephen sits in his train seat in an almost empty carriage.

A distant whistle. The train begins to pull away.

He reaches down, takes out the book that Hilary gave him. *High Windows*, by Philip Larkin.

He looks. There is a bookmark at page seven.

He turns to that page, and reads...

HILARY (V.O.)
The trees are coming into leaf
Like something almost being said;

182 EXT. PARK. DAY. 182

Hilary walks away from us through the tunnel of trees.

(CONTINUED)

182 CONTINUED: 182

HILARY (V.O.)
The recent buds relax and spread,
Their greenness is a kind of grief.

183 EXT. SEA FRONT. DAY. 183

Along the front, colourful bunting is hung everywhere, celebrating the wedding of Charles and Diana.

A crowd of kids watches a Punch and Judy show, shouting and cheering.

On the beach, an old attendant puts out the deckchairs for the day.

HILARY (V.O.)
Is it that they are born again
And we grow old? No, they die too.

184 INT. TRAIN CARRIAGE. DAY. 184

The English countryside flashes by outside the train window, as Stephen sits, reading the poem.

HILARY (V.O.)
Their yearly trick of looking new
Is written down in rings of grain.

185 INT/EXT. EMPIRE. DAY. 185

The empty rooms of the Empire.

The lobby. The screen. The abandoned ballroom.

Looking from the seafront - the Empire Cinema stands glinting in the sun.

HILARY (V.O)
Yet still the unresting castles
thresh
In full grown thickness every May.

186 EXT. SEAFRONT. DAY. 186

Hilary stands leaning up against the railing, looking out across the beach.

Norman stands alongside her. Neil arrives with a cup of tea.

(CONTINUED)

186 CONTINUED: 186

HILARY (V.O)
Last year is dead, they seem to
say,

Close on Hilary, the wind in her hair.

HILARY (V.O) (CONT'D)
Begin afresh, afresh, afresh.

She smiles, and looks out to sea.

END

Printed in Great Britain
by Amazon

17166891R00075